NOT
A
CHANCE

RECOLLECTIONS OF A
GLOBAL AMBASSADOR FOR CHRIST

DOUG CARTER

Copyright ©2020 Doug Carter
Not a Chance: Recollections of a Global Ambassador for Christ / Doug Carter

Published by Dust Jacket Press

ISBN: 978-1-947671-85-0

All rights reserved. No portion of this publication may be reproduced, stored in a retrieval system, or transmitted in any form or by any means, except for brief quotations in printed reviews, without prior permission of Doug Carter. Requests may be submitted by email: doug.carter@iequip.org

Dust Jacket Press
P. O. Box 721243
Oklahoma City, OK 73172
www.dustjacket.com

All Scripture quotations are taken from the King James Version of the Bible.

Dust Jacket logos are registered trademarks of Dust Jacket Press, Inc.

Cover and interior design: D. E. West / ZAQ Designs & Dust Jacket Creative Services

Printed in the United States of America

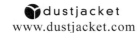

www.dustjacket.com

To Winnie Orvin Carter—

my sweet and beautiful wife,
my companion in life and ministry for sixty years,
faithful prayer warrior,
daily encourager,
and best mom and nana
on the planet.

———— ⚜ ————

Contents

Foreword.. vii

Introduction... ix

1. Childhood in Rockingham: 1941–1958................................ 1

2. From High School to Married Life: 1958–1964.................. 15

3. From Arizona to the Midwest to the World: 1964–2014..... 21

    Arizona to Ohio 44

    Taylor County Camp Meeting, Butler, Georgia.............. 59

    World Gospel Mission, Marion, Indiana 62

    EQUIP Leadership, Atlanta, Georgia 74

4. Global Ambassador for Christ: 2015–2020 105

5. Photo Gallery... 135

FOREWORD

I have known Doug Carter since the summer of 1983, when I had a fateful five-minute conversation with him around a church camp altar. As a seventeen-year-old boy with a calling to ministry, I was forever impacted in that moment by Doug's wisdom, godly passion, and wonderful charm.

As I wrestled with what serving the Lord might mean, Doug skillfully and lovingly opened my eyes to the vital importance of the fine ministry education at his school, Circleville Bible College, now known as Ohio Christian University. While saying yes to an education at this college was so meaningful for my future at that time, words fail me in expressing how monumentally important it has been to have Doug Carter in my life since that moment.

Doug has easily been the most consistently godly man I have ever known. His commitment to Christian service has been his daily passion for longer than I have been in the world. And his infectiously bright outlook lifts everyone, in every room he enters. And now, in serving with him at EQUIP Leadership and the John Maxwell Leadership Foundation, I am the envy of everyone who knows Doug—I get to be with him regularly!

Many roads in life may look the same, but the destinations may be quite different. And how different my destination would have been had I not intersected with Doug many years ago! That's why I fought for the chance to write the foreword to his delightful memoir, *Not a Chance*. In this book Doug Carter, master storyteller, beautifully recounts the incredible story of his life as an ambassador for Christ to the nations. With wonderful wit, beautiful prose, and careful reflection Doug skillfully describes the many roads he has taken as a faithful follower of Christ.

And now after decades of faithful service impacting multiplied thousands of lives, the destination is a masterpiece: by God's grace, Doug Carter didn't just travel the world—he transformed it! And while this book tells much of that story, the complete story of God's impact through Doug will be known only in heaven.

If you're like me, *Not a Chance* will challenge you to work harder, dig more deeply, serve longer, and be better in honor of the One who gave His all for each of us.

Now make no mistake—Doug is far from done. But he has written *Not a Chance* to challenge all who would come after him to say yes to God's grand design for their lives. What big thing in God's plan for your life might tempt you to say, "Not a chance"? Doug's life is proof that there is no limit to what God can do with a life totally surrendered to Him and to His purposes.

Read *Not a Chance* and ask yourself where you need to follow God more closely, more generously, and more committedly. Read this book and I know you will feel just like me—I am so glad I spent that time with Doug Carter!

—R. D. Saunders
Director of Advancement
EQUIP Leadership, Inc.

INTRODUCTION

The book you are about to read has been written throughout my lifetime. In fact, the first section was written for a class assignment when I was a junior in high school in the small rural community of Alma, Georgia. The other three sections were penned at different points in my life. As you read this book, I want you to see God taking an ordinary man on an extraordinary adventure of faith and obedience.

Quite frankly, when I penned the words that fill this book, my intended audience was my family and closest friends. I primarily wanted my grandchildren to have the opportunity one day to read the story of God's amazing faithfulness to a lad who at age eleven watched his father die. I wanted them to hear the story of how God used some amazing people to invest in my life, to help bring God's healing to my broken heart, and to believe in me when I had absolutely no belief in myself.

I was a teenager when my pastor, Rev. M. J. Wood, said to me, "Doug, in the future you will teach and preach all over the world." *Not a Chance*, the title of this book, are the words I whispered to myself in response to his unbelievable statement. After all, who could have believed that a shy, heartbroken lad from rural Georgia would eventually preach and teach the gospel in one hundred twenty-eight nations? I am forever grateful to my praying mother, my faithful pastor, and scores of others who have lovingly and faithfully invested in me. At each step on the journey a key person was there to add immense value and blessing to my life. Stan Toler, John Maxwell, Burnis Bushong, Ray Lyne, Karen Hartman, and Michel Khalil are only a few highlighted here.

The subtitle, *Recollections of a Global Ambassador for Christ*, was inspired by a comment made by Mark Smith, president of Columbia International University, when he introduced me to speak in chapel. He commented that many words could be used to describe the guest speaker. "The best word is *ambassador*—'global ambassador for Christ.'" He then terribly exaggerated when he referred to me as a "modern-day St. Paul." That was overstatement at its worst. However, the "global ambassador for Christ" label resonated. Whether I have been preaching the gospel, teaching biblical leadership principles, raising millions of dollars for kingdom ministry, or personally mentoring a promising young leader, it has always been the passionate desire of my heart to be a genuinely authentic representative of Jesus, my Savior and Lord.

Most of the book is devoted to the stories of men and women whom my wife, Winnie, and I have met around the world. We have faithfully endeavored to serve them well. But quite frankly, their lives of dedication, courage, and sacrifice as they serve Jesus in dark, difficult, dangerous, and often despised places have inspired, challenged, and stretched our hearts and drawn us closer to our Lord. I pray that their stories will strengthen your faith and ignite in you a renewed passion to make Christ known to the lost, the last, and the least.

Finally, please note that I have dedicated this book to my sweet and beautiful wife. I fell in love with Winnie Orvin when we were high school classmates back in the 1950s. On May 7, 1960, she became my wife. For six decades now we have been together on this journey of faith and obedience. We've served together, prayed together, wept together, and celebrated together. As Mom and Dad, Nana and Papa, and global ambassadors, we affirm that our highest aspiration has been Spirit-filled lives bearing the fruit of the Spirt of Christ so consistently that others would see the beauty of Jesus in us. It is my prayer that you will see Jesus in the pages of this book.

1

Childhood in Rockingham
1941–1958

*(This chapter was written in May 1958 at age
sixteen and a half, when I was nearing completion of my
junior year at Bacon County High School, Alma, Georgia.
The last paragraph was modified slightly.)*

I was born December 3, 1941, in the rural community of
Rockingham, Georgia, located about three miles east of
Alma, the county seat of Bacon County, Georgia. My father,
Floyd Carter, was a rural letter carrier, and my mother, Vera
Douglas Carter, was a housewife at the time of my birth. I was
born four days before the Japanese attack on Pearl Harbor.

I had two older sisters, Marguerite and Mary Kathryn, and
an older brother, James M. (Buddy). All three were already
married and away from home when I was born. Three years
after my birth, my baby sister, Johnnie, was born.

Going back to 1926, in that year United States President
Calvin Coolidge appointed my dad as postmaster for the Rock-

ingham, Georgia, post office; however, this office was merged with the post office in Alma a few years before I was born.

In 1941 Rockingham still had a train depot served by freight and passenger trains. There were three general stores where a quarter dollar would purchase a Coke, a pack of peanuts, and provide you a dime as change.

My first day in school was in September 1947. My parents, my younger sister, and I lived a short walk from the campus of Rockingham Elementary School. My first-grade teacher, Mrs. L. N. Johnson Sr., was a gracious Southern lady who served her Lord and loved her students. The principal was Chris Hyers. We learned the ABCs first; then we received our first book, titled *Mac and Muff*. Most of the kids had to bring a sack lunch, but I could walk home for lunch and enjoy Mom's delicious cooking.

After my first three weeks of school, my hands became infected with some strange disease, causing me to be out about three months. I visited several doctors, and one of them stated that my hands were in serious danger of permanent damage. Slowly, however, they began to heal. I returned to class and passed at the head of my class. I will never forget how much Mrs. Johnson helped me to catch up with my schoolwork after missing so many weeks of class. She was wonderful!

I was eager to start second grade. My teacher, Mrs. Doyle Crosby, was a stern disciplinarian. She wasn't much fun, but my reading and writing rapidly improved. Mr. Ammons, a very friendly and kind elderly gentleman, was our principal. Even though Rockingham was a public school, we had chapel every Friday morning. Mr. Ammons shared a lesson from the Bible and led us in prayer.

Mrs. Winton Murphy, my third-grade teacher, was a superb instructor. I consistently made the academic honor roll, which was printed in the school newspaper each grading period.

My mom insisted that I take piano lessons. That didn't last long. I had no love for music; instead, I totally loved sports. Nevertheless, our class did have a band, and we made our own instruments. For example, the drums were made from old nail kegs with inner tubes stretched over each end. One night we presented a concert for the whole community, and I was selected to be the band director. What a laugh! I did not know one musical note from the other—but neither did the band members!

I made all As throughout the third grade, but early in the fourth grade I encountered multiplication tables. I struggled for a few weeks but soon decided to buckle down and learn them. Once I mastered them I developed a real love for math.

My first and last playground fight was with a pastor's son who later became a dear friend. Both of us expected Mr. Ammons to use his paddle on us, for we deserved it. Instead, he gave us a long lesson on good behavior using a generous selection of Bible verses.

We played baseball at recess and during lunch hour. Because we were often short on the number of boys needed to fill a team, several of the girls also played. We played basketball on an outdoor dirt court.

Mr. and Mrs. H. H. DeWeese were my teachers for grades five through seven. I remember Mrs. DeWeese as one of the best teachers ever. While she was a great example of excellence in the classroom, I recall her as a special friend and as the teacher who instilled in me a love for English grammar. I still love diagramming sentences.

On the day before I entered the sixth grade, my father fell in the Alma post office and broke his right leg. He was rushed to a hospital in Augusta, Georgia, where he stayed for almost four months wearing a cast from his waist down with two metal pins through his leg. When he finally came home from the hospital in early December, he was still in a cast but seemed to be improving. However, on December 24, 1952, Christmas Eve, at 4:30 in the morning, he died from a blood clot.

That was a Christmas I'll never forget, the only sad one I can recall. The pain in my heart was intense. During the time when everyone should have been celebrating the joy of Christmas, our home was filled with only tears of grief, heartbreak, and sorrow.

I returned to school after Christmas with a very troubled heart, feeling terribly alone. My mom prayed daily for God to heal my heart, and my pastor offered comforting words. My teachers, Mr. and Mrs. DeWeese, did all they could to encourage me. I decided to work hard in class as a gift to my dad, confident that he was watching me from heaven. I earned all As for the entire year.

The seventh grade was my last at Rockingham. All the schools in Bacon County were being consolidated into one large school in Alma. Country schools like Rockingham would never again be filled with the sights and sounds of children. I was disappointed to see this happen to my beloved school. I finished my years at Rockingham School in May 1954. I can honestly say that every year at Rockingham was a pleasure and an adventure.

The eighth grade was quite a new adventure—I had six teachers and made many new friends. Mrs. Head was my favorite eighth-grade teacher.

By the time I entered high school in 1955, only one general store remained in Rockingham, located at the intersection of State Route 32 and Dedge Farm Road. Also, trains no longer ran through Rockingham, but I'll never forget the loud sound of the train whistle as the huge and powerful coal-fired, steam-powered locomotives chugged along with many boxcars and a dozen or so flatbeds in tow. The flat cars were loaded with large wooden logs headed to the paper mills on the coast.

Most all homes in Rockingham were built on either the north or south side of the railroad tracks, which divided the community. The homes faced each other across the tracks. Directly across the tracks from our house was the home of my dad's older brother, affectionately known as "Uncle Doc." Every home had a large front porch with rocking chairs and usually a swing. Many hot, muggy summer evenings were spent on the porch praying for even a gentle breeze. No one had air conditioning in those days. Everyone was grateful when the "ice man" arrived with blocks of ice to cool the icebox, where we kept perishable food items. Sweet iced tea was our favorite beverage—three times per day!

The back porch of the house was where the tubs and scrub boards were located for doing laundry. My mom often expressed gratitude for the day when electricity was brought to the Rockingham community for the first time. The washboards were replaced by Maytag washing machines with wringers, two rollers used to squeeze excessive water from clothes before they were placed on the outdoor clothesline for drying.

Also located on the back porch was the brooder, the small pen used for rearing baby chicks. When they were large enough to make it on their own, they were released into the fenced-in chicken yard. My mom was a fabulous cook, and nothing was more delicious than her fried chicken. I always felt a little sorry for the chicken in the barnyard that she selected for dinner. After wringing its neck, she scalded it in very hot water, plucked the feathers, thoroughly cleaned it, cut it into appropriate pieces, and placed the pieces into the cast-iron skillet filled with extremely hot grease. When she had removed the last piece of golden-brown chicken from the skillet, she used the drippings as the key ingredient in delicious gravy to be served over rice or mashed potatoes. Frankly, I loved the gravy best on grits, also known as "Georgia ice cream."

We had electricity in our home by the time of my birth; however, our toilet was an outhouse located quite a long walk behind our home (more on that in just a moment). Immediately behind the house was the smokehouse, where meat was cured and preserved using salt. The chicken house and the fenced-in chicken yard were behind the smokehouse. It was in this yard that my mom's leg was badly slashed by a rooster with one of his spurs. Nearby was the pigpen where the pigs were fed food scraps. Farther from the house were the barn and barnyard, where the old mule, Kate, and a few milk cows were kept.

The outhouse, noted above, was located near the barn. In this outhouse my mom was once frightened almost to death by a black snake. It was surely a joyful day when we got indoor plumbing and an indoor bathroom!

I recall that one of the sows died shortly after giving birth to thirteen pigs. Mom decided that we would raise the pigs on milk using nursing bottles and nipples. My little sister, Johnnie, and I fed them at least twice each day. We wanted to bring the smallest pig, called the runt, into the house for our pet, but Mom quickly vetoed that idea.

Kate, the aged mule, was very gentle with a slow gait. We smaller kids loved to ride in the wagon as Kate slowly pulled it along the unpaved roads of the Rockingham community. I recall one day when I, being the oldest of the kids, decided to ride Kate bareback to impress the younger children. When I climbed onto her back and reached for the reins of the bridle, she quickly and unexpectedly started running. I did an unplanned somersault onto the ground behind her, landing on my head. I'm quite sure from the lick on my head that I suffered a mild concussion. I still recall the nausea I felt after the accident. Of course, the nausea could have been the result of the humiliation I experienced as the younger children laughed loudly at me. Needless to say, that ended my career as a mule rider.

All us kids were great horseback riders so long as the horse was a stick with a rope or string tied to it as the bridle. We were all cowboys at one time are another—some the good guys and others the bad guys. The Long Ranger, Cisco Kid, Gene Autry, Roy Rogers, Jessie James, Billy the Kid, and many others rode in our imaginations. Occasionally my sister Johnnie would show up as Dale Evans. Frequently the bad guys would rob the stagecoach—Johnnie's doll carriage!

Ninth grade was my first year at Bacon County High School—a new building, perhaps the most modern in our state. In the spring of my freshman year I began playing football. Football is a rough sport, but I loved it. It is a lot of fun and helps develop a player physically and mentally. I played right tackle on offense and also on the defensive line.

I made all As during my ninth year in school, a record I would maintain throughout my years in high school. During the summer months of my high school years, I spent most of the time living with my brother, Buddy; his wife, Nadine; and their three children, Jimmy, Jerry, and Linda. Jimmy and Jerry were just a little younger than me. We worked together every day on my brother's farm. The work was difficult and the days were long. There is nothing quite like a hot, humid summer day in southeast Georgia! His two sons and I learned so very much about life as we worked together on the farm. A trip to Fernandina Beach, Florida, at the end of the summer was quite a reward for our countless hours of toiling under the miserably hot sun in the Deep South.

There were many difficult tasks on the farm, but I am sure harvesting tobacco and picking cotton were the most challenging. I recall countless days cropping tobacco, the process of removing or breaking several large leaves from the tobacco stalk. The cropper walked between the rows of tobacco stalks, which were well over six feet tall. The summer heat often reached one hundred degrees with about ninety-percent humidity on most days. The stalks and large leaves blocked any breeze that might have existed. Green, gooey tobacco tar covered the hands and arms of the cropper.

Picking cotton was equally difficult as one crawled between the rows of cotton and handpicked the locks of cotton and then placed them into a large burlap bag the picker towed behind him or her. Again, the sun was brutally hot. Even though a day of hard work in the tobacco patch or cotton field paid very little, I knew I could earn enough that by the end of summer I could buy my school clothes for the new school year. I consistently worked hard and endeavored to do my best. I always remembered my dad's words spoken to me several years before: "Son, if you'll always discipline yourself, no one else will ever need to."

We labored hard, for sure, and there were some special rewards. Like my mom and my sisters, my sister-in-law, Nadine, was a great cook and made fabulously delicious biscuits. They were so large that we called them "cathead" biscuits, and they were culinary masterpieces. There was no eating experience more wonderful than one of her biscuits straight from the oven, sliced open and covered with real butter and fresh homemade strawberry jam. As the hot butter and jam melted, it was such a delight to consume the biscuit with the melted butter and jam flowing down your arm and dripping off your elbows! That was a maximum eating experience.

Occasionally on Saturday evening we used the old hand-propelled churn to make a batch of delicious ice cream. There's nothing quite as delicious as homemade peach ice cream to cap off a long week of work on the farm in the summertime.

I spent many days chopping wood for the wood-burning stove in the kitchen and for the fireplaces in the family home in Rockingham. I celebrated joyfully when the old stove was replaced with an electric one.

Even with all the days of work in the fields, chopping wood, and taking care of Mom's vegetable garden, there were still occasional days to join with neighborhood kids swimming in the nearby creek, catching a few fish, or playing baseball or football on the unpaved road that ran in front of our house.

I was blessed to have several nephews who were close to my age. In fact, five of them were within three years of my age—Jimmy and Jerry (my brother Buddy's sons), Harry and Larry (my sister Marguerite's twin boys) and Benny (my sister Mary Kathryn's oldest son). You can only begin to imagine the fun we had on those occasions when all of us could be together in Rockingham. My little sister, Johnnie, was the youngest of the group. I don't think she greatly enjoyed having to play with boys only, but she always insisted on tagging along. She was quite a trooper!

As my tenth-grade year unfolded, I continued with excellent grades and dreamed of membership in the Beta Club, a society of academically top students. When the names were posted for Beta Club induction, however, my name was not on the list, and I was heartbroken. One of my teachers, convinced that a mistake had been made, hurried to the office to inquire about my name. He discovered that my name had been mistakenly placed on the list of seniors. I was a sophomore. The error was corrected quickly, and I was soon active in the Beta Club.

In March we traveled to Atlanta for the Beta Club convention and stayed at the Clermont Hotel in Druid Hills. Druid Hills High School had defeated our team for the boys' state basketball championship just days before in a game in a very controversial finish. The Druid Hills students were not very happy when we asked them if we could see *our* trophy. They didn't like us, and we were not particularly fond of them.

The convention banquet took place in the beautiful, historic Dinkler Plaza Hotel in Atlanta, and our club presented a short play in the talent contest. We were shocked to find six forks beside our plates and had no clue what to eat with each. One fork had always been adequate for us down in south Georgia. Atlanta seemed so far from home and such a strange place.

In August 1957 I attended football camp at Moody Air Force Base near Valdosta, Georgia. Wow! Those days were terribly hot and humid. We practiced football for six hours each day and had our meals in the mess hall with the servicemen. I think I lost fifteen pounds due to the heat.

I genuinely loved my eleventh year in school. Miss Betty Sue Jackson was my wonderful English teacher (she would soon become Mrs. R. T. Johnson). Words can never express how very much I enjoyed her class. While I always enjoyed school, she ignited in me a greater passion to learn. Mrs. Johnston, our typing teacher, was tough, but her talks, sayings, and quotes were a blessing and inspiration to me. The football season went well, and I loved the great meals following the road games. Beta Club Convention was again in Atlanta. This time we visited many of the interesting and historic sites in Georgia's capital city.

When the time arrived for the junior class to begin preparing to host the senior class for the annual Junior-Senior Banquet, a planning committee came up with the theme and the program. The junior class was responsible for all the hard work to get ready for the banquet, but a handful of us did most of the work. Miss Spell was our overseer and inspiration as she worked side by side with us evening after evening. She was an amazing class sponsor!

The banquet was held on Friday night, May 9, 1958. Winnie Orvin was my date, and we had a great time. She was very friendly with a beautiful smile and was a basketball player for the high school girls' varsity team.

Being very shy, I simply had not possessed the boldness to ask Winnie to be my date for the banquet. I just could not muster up the courage to risk the possibility that she would turn me down. One of my classmates in a math class was Eleanor, Winnie's sister. When I realized that Eleanor was struggling with the class—a class she was required to pass if she were to remain on the basketball team—I had an idea. Knowing she was a star player and eager to retain her academic eligibility, I made her an offer: "Eleanor, I'll help get you an A in math if you'll get me a date with your sister Winnie." She gladly accepted my proposal. She got an A—and I got a date with the girl of my dreams!

I was now looking forward to my senior year in high school. I had been elected an officer of the Beta Club and selected to serve on the yearbook staff. Later in the summer I would represent my high school at Boys' State Convention in Atlanta, where we would study government and politics.

2

From High School to Married Life
1958–1964

(Note: This chapter was written in 1964.)

When my father died in December of 1952, my mother assumed that the United States Post Office Department would provide monthly support for her and her two minor children. It was clear in my mom's mind that my dad's death was the result of an injury he had sustained on the job. The post office denied her claim for compensation.

Our pastor, Rev. M. J. Wood, would not accept the decision of the post office and for the next six years waged a battle with them. He wrote hundreds of letters to the U. S. Post Office Department, the U. S. Department of Labor, the Civil Service Commission, members of the U. S. House of Representatives and Senate, and U. S. President Dwight Eisenhower. He submitted hundreds of documents from doctors and hospitals in support of his position that my dad's death was a result of an injury sustained on the job due to the negligence of the post office. In May 1958 my mother received a letter from the U. S. Department of Labor stating, "The Bureau has found your husband's death was caused by the injury he sustained on September 1, 1952. Therefore, this office will pay compensation for death to the eligible dependents."

Our debt to Brother Wood for his determination and tenacity in making sure justice was done for a widow and her two minor children can never be paid. We are forever grateful. Only heaven can reveal the hours he invested in our behalf.

In the summer of 1958 I attended Taylor County Camp Meeting, where Pastor Wood served as camp president. It was in the rustic tabernacle in a Saturday morning service as Don Rollings sang "The Love of God" that I responded obediently to the pleading of the Holy Spirit and surrendered my life fully to Christ. Obedience to the Lord brought glorious victory!

I entered my senior year of high school in the fall of 1958 with high expectations, and what a year it would be! In the spring of 1959 Winnie Orvin would help lead her team to the state high school girls' basketball championship—shooting the winning free throw!

The story of the 1958–1959 Red Raiderettes basketball team should be made into a movie. Just prior to the beginning of the basketball season in the fall of 1958, the old wooden gymnasium at Bacon County High School burned to the ground. The team practiced outdoors when weather permitted and inside a tobacco sales barn or warehouse on cold, windy, or rainy days. They played every game of the regular season without a home game. Yes, every game was played away from home—regular season, regional playoff, and district and state tournaments. The Class AA State Championship game was played in the coliseum in Macon, Georgia, on a Saturday evening. The girls from Bacon County under the tutelage of Coach R. T. Johnson defeated Warner Robins High School by a score of 49–48 in a thriller! Winnie made the winning free throw with seconds on the clock. The headline on the first page of the sports section of the state's largest newspaper read, "From Tobacco Warehouse to State Championship!"

As our senior year neared an end, Winnie and I had begun dating regularly. She and I had fallen deeply in love and knew we wanted to spend the remainder of our lives together. Winnie had given her heart to Christ during revival services that spring of 1959. The guest evangelist was Rev. B. O. Crowe, from Marion, Indiana.

A couple of weeks after the revival services were concluded, it was time for the annual missions conference at our church. The missionary scheduled to speak for the conference was Don Hawk. He and his wife and family served as missionaries with World Gospel Mission in Honduras. One Wednesday evening at prayer meeting, one of the farmers in our church was praying for the upcoming missions weekend. He prayed, "Dear Lord, very soon Brother Crowe will be with us, or perhaps it will be Brother Hawk. Lord, whatever the bird's name is, would You please bless him?"

Winnie and I had so many mutual values. We loved the Lord, enjoyed serving Him, loved church, and desired to make an eternal difference in the lives of others. We enjoyed working hard and always endeavored to do our best with every responsibility given to us at work and at church. We enjoyed sports, Southern gospel music, and country music. Elvis was just beginning to introduce the world to "rockabilly" music.

We were blessed to have experienced our teenage years during the "happy days" of the 1950s. World War II had ended, and one of the war heroes, Dwight "Ike" Eisenhower, was our president. John Wayne and Marilyn Monroe were Hollywood stars. In 1959 a religious movie titled *Ben Hur* won an Oscar for best movie. The star, Charlton Heston, was honored as best actor. Superman was standing for truth, justice, and the American way.

We graduated from high school together as I was honored as class valedictorian. Winnie was one of the most popular students ever at Bacon County High School. Today she still loves God, people, and life—and she loves me. Wow—I am a blessed man!

As noted early, I was deeply wounded emotionally when my dad died on Christmas Eve morning in 1952. I was only eleven. I struggled to understand how God could love me while still having "taken" my dad from me. As a result of my hurt and pain, I tended to withdraw from most social interaction and became very quiet and reserved. I worked hard academically and endeavored to obey my mom, but it wasn't until several years later that I fully realized that God loved me and had a plan and purpose for my life. Ultimately it was the love of a godly mother, the prayers of a great local church family, and the unwavering care and support of a devoted pastor that convinced me that God loved me.

Shortly after I learned that I would graduate at the top of my high school class, the principal informed me that I would be required to give a speech during the commencement activities. About the same time, Pastor Wood told me that he was expecting me to speak to our church on the Sunday prior to graduation. This was a double whammy! I was scared almost to death with the thought of speaking to a crowd—two crowds! I insisted that I could not do either. The more I thought about it, the more I became literally sick. I thought I would need to be hospitalized.

When I told Pastor Wood that I could not speak to the church, he replied, "Yes, you can! One day you will teach and preach all over the world." As mentioned in the introduction to this book, when I heard his words I whispered to myself, "Not a chance." Brother Wood helped me prepare my sermon and stood beside me as I shared my testimony with the congregation gathered in our church. The Holy Spirit used my words to call many to salvation at the conclusion of that service. That experience helped prepare me to give my graduation speech.

Winnie and I were married May 7, 1960, in Alma, Georgia, with Pastor Wood officiating. We were both employed in

Alma, and I attended college classes evenings and weekends in Waycross. I will forever be grateful to my brother-in-law Hoke Carter, who gave me my first full-time job. Each day working with him was like attending graduate classes in business administration. I learned volumes about business, leadership, and working with people. Also, we became heavily involved in a variety of volunteer roles in our local church, the Evangelistic Temple in Alma.

3

From Arizona to the Midwest to the World
1964–2014

(Note: This chapter was written in April 2014.
Hundreds of godly men and women have played a crucially
important role in the lives of Winnie and me. I regret that
I am unable to mention all of them in this short narrative.
Those who go unmentioned have had no less influence
than those who are named.)

In 1964 Winnie and I entered missionary service with World Gospel Mission and began ministering to Native Americans in Arizona.

The passion in our hearts to reach this people group with the gospel burned as brightly as the noonday sun in Arizona. We knew God had called us to pour our lives into Native American children and youth who resided each school year at Southwest Indian School. We could hardly wait for the new school year, when we could begin our service as mom and dad to fifty American Indian boys from fourteen different tribes.

These lads, ranging in age from five to nineteen, would be under our care in Conover Dormitory.

Before the youngsters arrived for classes in late August, I was assigned the unenviable task of tearing down and removing an old storage shed on the campus. As I pulled up the final pieces of the rotten wooden flooring, hundreds of scorpions scurried in every direction. Welcome to life in the Arizona desert. (I'll provide more details a little later.)

What would bring a young couple from Georgia to Arizona to serve as missionaries? Why would we leave good jobs and active roles in our home church? Much of the "blame" can be placed squarely upon the shoulders of our pastor, Rev. M. J. Wood. It was he who resolutely insisted that the Evangelistic Temple in Alma, Georgia (now First Church of the Nazarene), be a church where the "whole counsel of God" is faithfully taught and the Great Commission mandate is the priority. Outstanding evangelists and missionaries from many nations were frequent speakers at our church. My mom, though working very hard as a single mom trying to provide for two children, hosted most of these servants of the Lord in our home. Two of my favorites were missionary-evangelist Jimmy Lentz and his lovely wife, Kitty. His stories from the mission fields around the world touched Winnie and me deeply. His stories are one of the main reasons I still love to share stories of how God is changing lives around the world.

Pastor Wood and his wife strongly encouraged my mom to attend the Taylor County Camp Meeting. He had founded the camp meeting in 1939 in a rural area of Taylor County, Georgia, a few miles north of Butler and about one hundred sixty miles northwest of Alma. My little sister, Johnnie, and I accompanied Mom to camp meeting in 1953, the first summer following the death of our dad. The children and youth services under the direction of Don and Jean Rollings had a major positive impact upon our lives. The evangelists were some of the best communicators ever, and the missionaries stretched our hearts to love the peoples of the world.

After Winnie and I married in 1960, she, too, became a regular at Taylor County Camp Meeting. We also attended the Gaskin Springs Camp Meeting, located only about twenty-five miles west of Alma. In the summer of 1963 Winnie and I—she at Gaskin Springs and I at Taylor County— answered yes as we heard God speaking to us about investing our lives in cross-cultural Great Commission ministry. World Gospel Mission missionaries Johnny and Peggy Miller, as well as Pastor Wood, Jimmy Lentz, and Clayton Luce, were mightily used of God to bring us to this point of obedience.

Shortly after camp meeting ended in the summer of 1963, Winnie and I began the application process to become career missionaries with World Gospel Mission. One afternoon while I was filling out one of the application forms, I was suddenly aware that the Holy Spirit was speaking to me about reading John 15:16. As I read the following words, I knew this verse would be a special treasure in my life from that day forward: "Ye have not chosen me, but I have chosen you, and ordained you, that ye should go and bring forth fruit, and that your fruit should remain: that whatsoever ye shall ask of the Father in my name, he may give it you."

Several years later a portion of another verse gave additional confirmation of God's calling upon my life: "Now then we are ambassadors for Christ" (2 Corinthians 5:20). I certainly didn't know at that time that I would eventually have the privilege and responsibility of representing Christ in many nations of our world.

Our applications for missionary service were approved in October 1963 by the Board of Directors of World Gospel Mission, Marion, Indiana. As missionaries with WGM, a "faith mission," it was necessary for us to raise our personal support team. During the first weekend of February 1964 I began engaging full-time in developing this team of prayer and financial partners by speaking in a church in Memphis. Winnie was invited to speak to the WGM Prayer Fellowship in Fort Valley, Georgia.

One of the very first individuals to pledge a monthly "share" in our ministry was Helen Luce, the wife of the founder of the Blue Bird Body Company, the largest school bus manufacturer in America, based in Fort Valley. In the years ahead many of the members of the Luce family would become some of our dearest friends and most generous and loyal supporters.

I was one of five children, and Winnie was one of ten. We wanted to have a large family. Sadly, multiple miscarriages would be our lot during our early years of marriage. A miscarriage takes a terrible toll emotionally. By the time our missionary appointments had been granted by WGM, we were beginning to lose hope of ever having children of our own. When we were informed that our first assignment on the field would be serving as "mom and dad" for fifty Indian boys, Winnie celebrated with great joy. She exclaimed, "I've been praying for one child, and God has given me fifty all at one time! Isn't God good?"

I'll never forget the drive from Alma, Georgia, to Glendale, Arizona, in the middle of July 1964. As I drove our 1960 automobile, towing all our earthy possession behind it in a small U-Haul trailer, the trek across west Texas seemed endless—and the car did not have air conditioning. As we drove through El Paso at high noon, the engine was overheating and Winnie and I were feeling the same, placing wet handkerchiefs across our faces to try fending off the terrible heat. As we drove into Las Cruces, New Mexico, in early afternoon, the radio announced the local temperature at one hundred fifteen degrees. Winnie begged me to stop at a motel for rest and respite from the heat, reminding me that we had driven about thirty hours without rest.

When we stepped into our air-conditioned sleeping room at the little Travelodge hotel, we felt we had arrived in paradise. No palatial resort on earth could have been more wonderful. We slept about ten hours before resuming our journey, which then took us across New Mexico and on to the Phoenix Valley. As we drove down Grand Avenue in Glendale, only a few miles from Southwest Indian School, a huge sign on Don Sanderson Ford proclaimed that the temperature was one hundred nineteen degrees!

After getting settled into our mobile home on the campus of Southwest Indian School, I was given my first assignment, noted earlier: tearing down a very old storage shed located in the center of the campus. With the temperature about one hundred fifteen degrees in the shade, I ripped away the rotten lumber as quickly as possible. As I began lifting the wooden flooring, I noticed little creatures scurrying from beneath the floor and across the yard. I quickly realized that hundreds of poisonous scorpions lived beneath the floor of that old shed. I had just made them very angry. I very carefully removed the remaining flooring while carefully avoiding contact with the agitated scorpions. Then I began the task of trying to kill them one by one as they ran across the yard in every direction. As I finished this very unpleasant task, I prayed that future assignments would prove more rewarding. I had no idea that just one year later, at age twenty-three, I would be chosen by my peers and the leaders of WGM to serve as the superintendent of the American Indian Field and Southwest Indian School.

When the tribal boys and girls arrived on campus in late August, we fell in love with them. There was never a dull moment! In addition to caring for the lads in our dorm, Winnie worked in the school's business office while I helped with maintenance chores and coached basketball, softball, baseball, and other sports. I usually had at least six teams, both boys and girls, during each season of the school year. As our first year at Southwest Indian School year concluded, we could report that forty-eight of our boys had made decisions to follow Christ!

Many of the students came from reservations located in desert areas, where the water supply was often quite limited. The students, especially the younger boys, loved the showers at the school, where warm, clean water was available in abundance. I recall one evening while the older boys were studying or perhaps outside playing ball, several of the younger boys went to take showers in the rather large room attached to the dormitory. I was reading a book and paid little attention to them. Suddenly I realized they had all been in the shower room a very long time. I had no idea that the boys had turned on all the showers and plugged the drains with their towels. As a result, the shower room had become a swimming pool. When I opened the door to check on the lads, a flood of water almost swept me off my feet. In the deluge of water were a dozen naked little brown-skinned boys. I wanted to punish them—but the escapade was far too creative for me to do anything but laugh.

The summer of 1965 would bring a major change to our lives. Rev. Earl Newton, the long-time director of WGM's American Indian Field and superintendent of Southwest Indian School, and his wife, Margaret, retired from missionary service that they had begun decades before in China. George Warner, president of WGM, missionary statesman, and former missionary to China, came to Arizona to conduct the election of the new director and superintendent. All the missionaries in Arizona who had completed at least two years of missionary service were eligible to cast votes. Winnie and I, having served only one year, were not permitted to vote nor were we eligible to hold a field office, such as director, treasurer, secretary, or member of the executive committee.

When the ballots for field director were counted, I had received all but one vote. Dr. Warner, always a gracious Christian gentleman, explained that there had been a misunderstanding. He kindly but firmly explained that under WGM policy I was not eligible to hold the director's position. He asked for a second ballot. This time around I received one hundred percent of the votes! Missionaries can be stubborn and independent! Dr. Warner described the situation as a "constitutional crisis" and adjourned the gathering so he could contact other members of the WGM administration for counsel.

After a delay of a couple of hours, Dr. Warner announced that an exception had been made and that I would be permitted to serve as field director and superintendent of the school. He stated that two assistant directors, both veteran missionaries, would be appointed to be my mentors. Noble Wilkinson, who began his missionary years in Kenya, and Mollie Hensley, a godly lady from North Carolina, became my faithful prayer partners and most loyal supporters. I am forever indebted to them for helping a twenty-three-year-old, the youngest member of the missionary team, successfully lead the school and the field for the next fifteen years. Spiritual victories, new buildings, a growing student body, and more missionaries and volunteers marked these years.

During our second year of missionary service on the American Indian Field, I was officially ordained to the Christian ministry by executives of World Gospel Mission. Warner and Hollis Abbott, vice president of field ministries, led the ceremony.

There was never a time during my tenure, from 1965 to 1980, when Southwest Indian School was not involved in a building project. Teams of volunteers came from across America to construct dormitories, classrooms, staff homes, a new chapel, and athletic facilities. The volunteers, the finances, and the government permits needed were often miraculously provided in answer to the prayers of missionaries, Indian students, many of their parents, and friends in numerous states. We lived a never-ending miracle as we daily experienced God's favor and blessing. The Lord seemed never to provide early—but never too late.

During one occasion when we were working on a large classroom building, on the very day the team of volunteer construction workers arrived the construction permit was granted and a check was received in the mail to cover the cost of the building materials! In addition to the expansion of the school, ministries were initiated on several Indian reservations in Arizona and New Mexico.

Both Men with Vision, a ministry of World Gospel Mission, and Missionary World Service and Evangelism (now known as GO International) brought dozens of volunteer work teams to our campus to help with building projects and maintenance and in countless other ways.

When 1968 rolled around, Winnie and I still did not have children of our own. We had pretty much concluded that the Indian boys and girls would be our only "family." But a very special miracle happened September 26, 1968—a beautiful baby daughter, Angela, arrived! Being in our ninth year of marriage at this time, surely you can understand our excitement, joy, and gratitude to God and to the many friends who had prayed for this miracle to happen.

When we brought our precious gift from God, Angie, to our home on the school campus, the first person to look into her face there was a lovely Navajo girl, Wanda Smallcanyon. As if in total surprise and shock, she exclaimed, "She's white!" Wanda was expecting a brown-skinned baby with dark eyes and a full head of black hair. She certainly didn't expect a pale-face with blue-green eyes and almost no hair! Winnie and Wanda became very close friends, and Winnie played an important role in leading Wanda to a vibrant relationship with Christ.

About five years after Angie's birth, she began praying every evening for a baby brother. We reminded her that her birth was nothing short of a miracle and that it could be that she would never have a brother or sister. She persisted in her praying, however—and on February 8, 1975, Eric Timothy was born. We had planned to call him Timothy, but some of the Indian boys objected that we were playing favorites by using the name Timothy. You see, they thought we were favoring Timothy Begay, a Navajo lad whom I had led to Christ and with whom I had developed a close friendship.

Then, when Jason Douglas was born on May 30, 1978, Winnie and I were quite content for the "baby miracles" to cease. After all, we were getting old! God had given us three miracle children—and what amazing blessings they continue to be in our lives!

Our children loved their childhood days on the campus of the Southwest Indian School. With a large number of MKs (missionary kids) and almost two hundred Native American children and youth as friends and playmates, they were never bored. Our children thought of the other missionaries as their aunts and uncles. Ron and Becky Brown, Art and Nancy Butler, and Don and Gail Norton were especially close to Angie, Eric, and Jason.

Eric played every day with his friend Nathan Brown. He loved visiting with him at his house. One day his "Aunt Becky" asked him to have lunch with Nathan. Eric was very excited when Winnie gave her okay for him to eat with Nathan. After only a few minutes we heard Eric entering the backdoor of our house. Big tears were flowing down his face. When his mom asked what was wrong, he exclaimed, "I don't like Aunt Becky's hotdogs!"

Winnie asked why, and Eric muttered, "Because they're not Oscar Meyer." That lad knew what he liked!

Winnie and I were always partners in ministry. She faithfully served the Lord in many roles during our sixteen years on the American Indian Field. Dorm mom, food service assistant, substitute teacher, field treasurer, bookkeeper, encourager, prayer partner, loyal friend, mom to three children, and godly wife are only a few of the roles in which she invested her life lovingly in others.

During our years at the school many of the graduates of the high school successfully matriculated to colleges and universities to continue their studies. Several of these students, Tim Begay and his sister Martha, Mike Andrews, Mike Martinez, Debbie Curley, Debbie Liston, Deanna Garcia, Frankie Yellowhorse, and others attended Circleville Bible College in Circleville, Ohio (now Ohio Christian University). The president of the college was Melvin Maxwell, father of John C. Maxwell. I developed a close friendship with Dr. Maxwell, perhaps because of our shared vision to see Native American youth reach their full potential as Christian leaders.

Winnie and I hold deep in our hearts the memories of so many special people with whom we served in Arizona. Noble and Eula Wilkinson, Ron and Becky Brown, Art and Nancy Butler, Erwin and Naomi Patricio, Maurice and Isabelle Woodworth, David and Sandra Oxedine, Don and Gail Norton, Mollie Hensley, Maxine Moss, Lois Major Ford, Les and Mary Ruth Madsen, Orville and Dortha Wilkinson, Oscar and Mildred Offett, Ruth Thorpe, Clair and Dorothy Lund, Lester and Sarah Pinkley, Karen Kornmiller, and scores of others enriched our lives and helped Southwest Indian School fulfill its God-given mission.

While many people touched our lives in profound ways, my friendship with Erwin Patricio and his family was one of the most impactful. Erwin grew up on the Papago Indian Reservation in southern Arizona. His grandfather introduced him to "firewater" (alcoholic beverages) when Erwin was only nine, and by early adulthood he was known as "the reservation drunkard." When he was introduced to Christ after years of sinful living, his life was powerfully transformed.

After only a few months of walking with Christ, Erwin knew God was calling him to preach the gospel. Following Bible college studies in New Mexico, he began pastoring a congregation in Navajoland. When I heard about his fruitful pastoral ministry, I went to meet him and to invite him to our campus to speak for revival services. Later it was my joy to ask him and his family to move to the campus of the Southwest Indian School to serve as our campus chaplain. His ministry on campus was mightily used of God to reach Native American youth for Christ. He would frequently say, "I'm an Indian by race but I'm a Christian by grace!" So many students, whatever their tribe, commented that they saw Jesus in the lives of Erwin and Naomi.

While we always endeavored to maintain a strong academic program at Southwest Indian School with a very large percentage of our graduates matriculating to colleges and universities, our highest priority was effective ministry to the spiritual needs of our students. Multiple chapel services each week, Sunday School classes for all grade levels, daily Bible studies in every classroom, devotional times in the dorms, and one-on-one times of prayer and counseling were only a few of the methods utilized to build relationships with our students, earn their trust, introduce them to Christ, and to help them become fully devoted followers of our Lord.

Our sports and music programs were vitally important tools for both evangelism and discipleship. Erwin Patricio, our campus chaplain, did much of the preaching for chapel services, yet some of his most effective ministry was in his role as a coach for the high school girls in several sports. Many of our missionaries and volunteers invested daily in our students through sports or music. While they produced many championship teams in numerous sports and filled the trophy case with beautiful awards, their priority was always to help develop young men and women into champions for Christ.

A high point of the sports program was winning the state championship in boys' basketball in 1976 in a hard-fought game played at Arizona State University. Our boys were not nearly as tall as the opposition players, but the Native lads were very fast and were superb shooters. Superior conditioning, full-court press on defense, and a fast-break offense wore down the taller, slower opponents. Cutting down the nets and standing in the winner's circle was the culmination of a long journey.

I well remember starting the basketball program back in the fall of 1964 with a few Native American lads who loved to play the game. We couldn't afford to buy uniforms for the boys, so Winnie dyed white T-shirts red. I used a black marking pen to add numbers to the shirts. When the boys stepped onto the court with their homemade uniforms, I never dreamed that in a few years another team from Southwest Indian School would win a state championship! There would be championships in other sports. I will always be grateful for Erwin Patricio, Don Norton, Maurice Woodworth, Jim Sizemore, and many others who understood the importance of using sports as a method of investing in young lives. I also hold in my heart precious memories of Johnny and Peggy Miller, Mary Ruth Madsen, Della Johnson, Tom James, and others who taught Native youth to sing hymns and songs of praise and worship.

Erwin, like most other Native American people, had a rather dry wit. I recall one morning when he and I were driving southward from Phoenix toward a reservation village located near the Mexico border. Erwin was quite desperate for a cup of hot, strong coffee. We parked at a truck stop and went inside. He asked the price of a cup of coffee, and the waitress replied that each cup cost fifty cents. Erwin then asked the cost of refills. The lady replied, "They're free."

Erwin replied, "My friend and I would like to order two refills."

One Saturday morning the high school boys' basketball team had played a very tough game in the Scottsdale area. After the lads won the hard-fought game, I decided to treat them at a local Mexican restaurant where a customer paid one price and could eat as much as possible, with no limits. This seemed a good plan for a group of very hungry young men. We sat at a large table filled with tacos, enchiladas, burritos, beans, rice, tortillas, and other items served family style. When a platter was low on food, a full platter replaced it.

I noticed an elderly Anglo (white) couple seated at a nearby table. They were carefully observing the enormous volume of food the Indian youth were consuming. Finally the gentleman walked slowly to our table and tapped one of the Navajo boys on the shoulder as he commented, "Young man, I wish I had your appetite."

The lad with a very slight grin and a twinkle in his eyes replied politely, "Wow! You took my land. You took my buffalo. Now you want my appetite!"

It was my privilege to invite evangelists, missionaries, and our campus pastors to speak for revival services and other special events. At Southwest Indian School and later at Circleville Bible College I endeavored to invite the very best communicators. Outstanding Native American speakers Fred Yazzie, Tom Claus, Allen Early, Alex Riggs, Joe Curley, Clarence Liston, and others preached the Word of God. Nationally known Christian leaders Jimmy Lentz, Stan Toler, Jonah Mitchell, Robert Morris, Delmer Ransdell, Charles Lake, Max Morgan, Delmus Hamilton, Don Rollings, Lu Smith, Burnis Bushong, Lee De-Saulnier, Owen Glassburn, Eddie Lockwood, and others ministered very effectively to our student body. Each was unique in one way or another.

Jimmy Lentz was one of the most gifted storytellers ever. I had first heard him back when I was a teenager. I loved the way he included stories in his sermons to illustrate key points. The stories were often about biblical characters, but many were stories from world history or current events, and some very humorous. As I listed to Brother Jimmy, I remembered that Jesus also told stories when He taught His disciples. As I've shared stories in my preaching and teaching around the world, I've realized the power of a story told well. It is quite obvious why stories are powerful. People learn from them. People love them. People remember them. People repeat them.

The wit and humor of Lee DeSaulnier will never be forgotten. His story about puncturing the aerosol can of whip cream with hammer and nail and the resulting "snowstorm" throughout his house evokes laughter every time I recall it. During the time Lee was on our campus an epidemic of mumps invaded the boys' dorm. The school nurse, Ruth Thorpe, declared the campus under quarantine with orders for no one to leave campus. When he preached his closing sermon on Sunday evening, Lee whispered to me, "Brother Doug, if you'll open the back gate to the campus, I'll drive out and be halfway to Los Angeles before Sister Thorpe misses me!" I must confess that I did help him "escape" the travel restriction.

One of the friendships we established while in Arizona was with David and Connie Dean. We first met them in the early 1970s when they were pastoring a church in Tucson. From the day we met, their love for the Lord and passion to reach the unsaved were beautifully obvious. The anointing of the Holy Spirit was clearly upon the Deans' lives and ministries. Their encouraging words and loving, caring deeds consistently inspired us. Year after year this friendship grew deeper and stronger. Our mutual friendship with Stan Toler and John Maxwell linked our hearts even more passionately in a shared vision to see our world reached for Christ.

When David and Connie and their infant daughter, Heather, left Arizona to pastor our home church in Alma, Georgia, we had no idea that our lives would be brought together closely in ministry just a few years later in Ohio. In various leadership roles, in local church ministry, and in Great Commission outreach around the world, we have served together in the joyful bonds of a truly special friendship.

In addition to our duties on campus at Southwest Indian School, I often visited Indian reservations throughout Arizona and in neighboring states. I frequently spent time visiting with parents of students enrolled at our school. Also, quite often I was invited to speak in churches located on reservations.

My first such experience happened when Rev. Joe Curley invited me to speak at his church, located on a Navajo reservation in Arizona. Pastor Joe and his lovely wife, Lillie, were both Navajos and very deeply committed servants of Christ. When I asked him the time of the Sunday morning service, he replied by lifting his arm at about a forty-five-degree angle. I surmised that he meant about midmorning, so Winnie and I dutifully arrived at about 10:00 the following Sunday morning. I remember driving across the desert on the long two-lane dirt road that ended in front of the rustic church building. No one appeared to be at the church. There were no horses or pickup trucks to be seen anywhere. I do recall that several sheep were wandering around in front of the church.

After Winnie and I waited in the car for almost two hours, we saw Pastor and Mrs. Curley arriving at the church. Many others arrived almost immediately thereafter, and very soon the church was filled with Navajos ranging in age from infants to the very elderly. After a lengthy time of congregational singing, prayer, and testimonies, Pastor Joe announced that one of the young men in the church had recently been called to preach and asked him to come forward and preach his first sermon. The sermon was quite long and doubled in length as it was interpreted into English for our benefit.

After the sermon came another long period of singing and testimonies. About 4:00 in the afternoon Brother Curley stated, "Brother and Sister Carter have driven all the way from Phoenix to be with us. I would like for him to come now and deliver the message of the morning." My message was interpreted into Navajo; thus, the service ended well past 5:00. Brother Curley invited everyone to gather behind the church to enjoy a dinner of delicious mutton stew. Yes, late that Sunday afternoon we ate the same sheep that had been milling around the church earlier in the day! Our beverage was hot Pepsi that had spent several hours under the brilliant Arizona sun.

I also recall clearly one of my first visits to the Hopi Indian Reservation, located in the very heart of Navajoland and fully encircled by the much-larger Navajo Reservation. The Hopi people live in several villages on the top of high mesas in the desert. The village of Orabi is considered the oldest continuously inhabited village in all of North America. I knew the parents of a Hopi student at Southwest Indian School, and they graciously invited me to visit their village.

As I strolled through the town I was invited to enter a pueblo where an aging Hopi elder was making pottery. I almost overlooked him as he sat in the corner of the room made of adobe clay. The walls were almost the same color as his skin tone. Without saying a word, he continued shaping the lump of clay that he held in his hands. Around me in the room I could see beautiful clay vessels sitting on rustic wooden shelves. I quickly realized that he was a master craftsman able to take a handful of dirt and transform it by the touch of his hands into a vessel of rare and exquisite beauty. After I stood for a long pause just to admire his artistry, I stepped outside and continued my tour of the village.

Eventually I was led to the edge of the mesa. I look into the distance and saw large fields of corn growing in the desert sand. I watched as several women of the village gathered the blue corn and ground it into corn meal. Then they filled large clay vessels with the corn meal while other women filled vessels of clay with water from a nearby deep well. Slowly the ladies walked up the long, winding trail back up to the village, where they went from pueblo to pueblo to share the corn meal and the water. It was quite apparent that many of the people, especially the elderly and infirmed, would have starved without the ground corn and water delivered to them. I decided that day that clay vessels in service making a difference are more beautiful than clay vessels sitting on the shelf simply looking pretty.

As I continued standing at the edge of the mesa, I looked straight downward. I was shocked to see what appeared to be thousands of pieces of broken pottery. I wondered why so many vessels had become fragmented, disjointed, and discarded on this huge trash pile.

I insisted on a return visit to the potter I had seen earlier. I entered his home and politely asked through an interpreter if he could explain why so many vessels were broken and on the garbage heap. He spoke slowly while explaining that he never intended for any of his pottery to become broken and worthless; he wanted every piece to be beautiful and valuable.

"But some of the clay was stubborn," he said. "It was hard and brittle and would not submit to my touch. When the finished product was tested in the fire, it came out broken. I had no choice but to toss it over the edge of the mesa and onto the discard pile." His words seemed to bring sadness to his face.

As I walked away from the pueblo, I thought about another potter, the Master Potter of all the ages. God the Creator long ago scooped up the clay of the ground and fashioned with His own hands His masterpiece of creative genius. He left his fingerprints on Adam, breathed into his nostrils the breath of life, gave him freedom of choice and moral accountability, and placed him in the garden.

But there was an outlaw in God's universe. Sin had been born in the pride and arrogance of Lucifer (Satan). God's enemy approached Adam and his wife, Eve, and began to plant seeds of doubt about God's goodness, integrity, and fairness.

Adam and Eve decided to disobey the Creator, who daily fellowshipped with them and lavished His love upon them. As a result of their disobedience, the outlaw in the universe became the outlaw in the human heart. Sin invaded and polluted their very nature. From that day forward every child of Adam's race has been born with the deadly disease of sin infecting his or her heart. The Bible declares, "In Adam all die" (1 Corinthians 15:22).

The Creator could have been finished with His stubborn, rebellious creature of clay; but because of His love and mercy, He had long before designed a plan of redemption and restoration for broken, discarded vessels. His promises of a coming Redeemer or Savior are seen throughout the Old Testament. Every book seems to shout, "The Deliverer is coming!" Then one glorious day John the Baptist exclaimed, "Behold the Lamb of God, which taketh away the sin of the world" (John 1:29).

Jesus, the God-man, willingly gave His life on the Cross in order to purchase the broken vessels of Adam's sinful race. For over two thousand years Jesus has been walking through the field of discarded vessels for whom He died. He looks down with tender mercy and invites worthless vessels to be made whole again.

I will never forget that Saturday morning when I reached up to Him in simple faith as a teenager and He reached way down into the pit and picked up the broken pieces of my life and miraculously made me whole. Subsequently His Spirit cleansed my heart and filled it to overflowing measure with

the Spirit of Him who is the Water of Life and the Bread of
Life. Since that day the desire of my heart has been to be a
clean vessel in faithful service sharing Jesus with a hungry and
thirsty world.

How can we ever forget the Indian young people who en-
deared themselves to us as if they were our own children? Debbie Curley and her siblings, Tim Begay and his sisters, Mike
Martinez and his brothers, Frankie and Elaine Yellowhorse,
Russell Trujillo, Danny Liston and his siblings, George and
Mae Willie, Ronald and Annabelle Smallcanyon, Irene Laughter, Wanda Smallcanyon, Deanna Garcia, Mike Andrews, Dale
and Charlotte Tsosie, Leroy DeJolie and his siblings, Roy Nells,
Chavis and Lillian Elliott, Linda Begay and her siblings, Dorothy Jim and her siblings, and scores of others were special gifts
from the Lord.

Transparency requires me to acknowledge that there were
difficult times when our missionary salaries were late in arriving. Yes, our compensation was small and sometimes late. It
was these days that drove us to our knees and to a greater de-
pendency on God as our supply and victory regardless of the
circumstances. Clothes for the children frequently arrived at
the moment of greatest need. My sister Marguerite was often
the one who purchased and sent the clothing. On one occasion Stan and Linda Toler, church-planters on a very limited
income, sent us fifty dollars. It arrived the day we were about
to cancel an urgently important doctor's appointment because
we didn't have a dime. Additionally, our home church in Alma

raised the funds to purchase us a car at a time when they did not know the old Ford was about to expire!

Arizona to Ohio

In the summer of 1980 Winnie and I were living for a few weeks in the home of Stan and Linda Toler in Ohio. Linda is my niece, and Stan was pastoring Heritage Memorial Church in Washington Court House, Ohio. Stan, who had begun investing in our ministry while he was still a student at Circleville Bible College, invited me to attend the General Council of our denomination, the Churches of Christ in Christian Union. While at General Council, several members of the board of directors of the college approached me about serving as president. Melvin Maxwell, who had presided over the college for sixteen years, had announced his resignation a few weeks before.

My answer to all such inquiries was pretty much the same: "God has called us to Arizona and to the Indians." However, deep in my heart I was beginning to believe that God doesn't call us to places and positions—rather, He calls us to a Person, His Son. If Jesus is truly our Lord, I believe He is free to send us to the places and positions of His choice. We obey Him as He gives direction and guidance.

Thus, in August 1980 I appeared before the committee leading the search for the new college president. Quite honestly I expected that another candidate, a friend I considered far more qualified than I, to be recommended to the full board by the search committee. I was ready to continue serving in

Arizona, but God had other plans—and I was unanimously recommended to the board of directors. Later the same day I met with the full board, sharing my testimony and discussing with them our shared vision for the future of the institution. With everyone voting affirmatively, I was invited to follow Dr. Maxwell as the president of Circleville Bible College. With confidence mingled with humility and an awareness of my own inadequacies, I accepted the position. It was a high honor and huge responsibility to succeed Dr. Maxwell, one of my spiritual heroes.

Earlier the same day in her quiet time, Winnie reminded the Lord of her desire to continue serving Him in Arizona but concluded her prayer with a statement of resolve to do His will and to follow Him wherever He led. The Holy Spirit gently revealed to her that Circleville Bible College was in our future. He also filled her heart with the peace that accompanies full surrender to His will—the peace that passes all human understanding.

I'll leave it to others to judge the results of our years at Circleville, but it was nine years of learning and growing for me. On my first day on the job I observed two places worn through the carpet beside the desk in the president's office. Upon inquiry about the damaged carpet, I learned that they were made by the knees of Dr. Maxwell as daily he prayed for the faculty, staff, and students in his care and under his leadership. Yes, moments like that stretched me in my walk with Christ and in my development as a servant-leader.

The opportunities to invest in the lives of God-called young men and women will forever be cherished. I'll never forget the countless hours with musical teams as we traveled together through many states. Also, I would frequently ask one of the young male students to travel with me to speak in a church or conference hours away from Circleville. As we engaged in conversation, it was a blessed privilege to pour into his life. Those were memorable mentoring experiences. I rejoice that many of those students became strong and effective servant-leaders who continue making an eternal difference as they invest their lives in others.

I turned forty December 3, 1981. My alarm clock was always set to awaken me with the morning news on the local radio station in Circleville. The second news headline caught my attention that morning: "We extend our condolences to Dr. Doug Carter, the president of Circleville Bible College. He goes over the hill today. There is a report that that a black flag is now flying on the flagpole in front of his office, and it is lowered to half-mast."

When I arrived at the campus that morning, the black flag was indeed waving in the breeze as a group of students approached my car with a wheelchair, expressing their sorrow that I had gone "over the hill." They wheeled me to my office, which was draped in black crepe paper. When I arrived at the local Rotary Club noon luncheon that pleasant Thursday in early December, the president announced in a mournful tone that the president of the local college was "over the hill and almost finished." Everyone had a big laugh and then expressed their condolences.

In the early afternoon I was informed that reservations had been made for Winnie and me to dine that evening at one of the very nice restaurants in Columbus. After a delicious meal and an unhurried time to reflect on the day, we drove home. When we arrived in our neighborhood at 9:30 in the evening, we noticed a large number of vehicles parked on our street. Winnie commented that one of the neighbors must he hosting a party of some sort. When we stepped into the kitchen from the garage, we heard a chorus of people yelling loudly, "Happy birthday!" When we entered the living room, it was packed with faculty, staff members, and other close friends. Right in the middle of the group stood Angie, Eric, and Jason grinning widely. They were so excited that they had helped to pull off successfully the surprise party to wrap up a most memorable fortieth birthday. I still think Jim Dorsey was the "brains" behind the whole day!

Throughout the history of CBC/OCU the music groups have effectively represented the school and the Lord Jesus in church services, camp meetings, and conferences. Scores of talented, Spirit-anointed young men and women have served the Lord in the college chorale, as well as in trios, quartets, and other groups. I loved traveling and ministering with them as often as possible. I often recall an incident in the summer of 1983 involving Maranatha, one of the singing teams. The group of six was traveling by van, towing a small trailer, from

Texas to Arizona when the driver fell asleep at the wheel. The following is an edited description of the accident as written by the driver:

My mind was in a daze as I drove fifty miles per hour up a steep hill. The next thing I knew, the hum of tires on the pavement was abruptly replaced by the noise created when driving on very rough terrain. Snapping out of my slumber, I found myself in a major crisis. The van and trailer had veered through the passing lane and were now diagonally in the median heading straight for an oncoming car!

I jerked the steering wheel until we were riding parallel to both roads. I slammed on the brakes, but they seemed to work so slowly in this moment when every fraction of a second and each decision that had to be made and then carried out could mean the difference between life and death.

It was apparent that the van was not going to stop before we hit the obstacle in the median, but trying to climb over it would be much too dangerous. I turned my wheel toward the right. Our route to the highway was up a shoulder that was high and steep, but there was no other option. The conditions thrust us airborne for several feet. My attempt to go straight ahead was spoiled when the trailer, filled with sound equipment, jackknifed and slammed against the side of the van. I was now content to end the skid with a sideways slide if we could remain upright, but we all knew a roll was inevitable.

The speed of the van and pull of the trailer lifted the driver's side off the ground. The sounds of crushing metal and shattering glass were soon added. Our bodies were helplessly tossed in random positions. We were totally at the mercy of the Lord.

After the roll there were six bodies lying on the ceiling of the van, which was now the floor of the van. My first thought was that the vehicle was about to explode. I was able to open my door. One of the other students helped everyone to climb out. Amazingly, we were all alive!

A registered nurse who had witnessed the accident quickly arrived on the scene. He was driving the oncoming vehicle that we almost hit. This "angel" took most of the group to a nearby house to regain their composure, care for a cut on the leg of one of the girls, and make a phone call to President Carter.

I'll never forget that phone call. The students seemed concerned about the van and the musical equipment. I had only one question: "Are all of you safe?" When they replied that the only injury was very minor, I began rejoicing and praising the Lord for His miraculous protection for the six young men and women who were investing their summer in service to Him. The 1983 Maranatha group continues having a very special place in my heart.

Graduates, administrators, board members, faculty, and staff of CBC/OCU became some of our dearest friends: David and Sally Case, David and Connie Dean, Mark and Lois Taylor, Robert and Ledie Kline, Raymond and Mildred Moats, R. D. and Shelli Saunders, Bret and Beth Layton, Bruce and Carmen Morrison, George and Susan Jones, Steve and Stephanie Schellin, Dwight and Patty Mason, Mike and Charla Holbrook, Mark and Bev Donohue, David and Tammy Gallimore, Ralph and Becky Hux, Jonah and Donna Mitchell, David and Myrla Lattimer , Paul and Mary Kay Manning, Larry and Bonnie Olson, Steve and Rose McGuire, Terry and Lois Miller, Jim and Rhonda Dorsey, Dan and Pam Schafer, Linda Long Cozad, Chuck Elliott, and scores of others.

During the years we lived in Circleville, Stan and Linda Toler and their two boys, Seth and Adam, lived about a thirty-minute drive from us in Washington Court House. Our children, Angie, Eric, and Jason, loved to visit the Toler family. In fact, they thought a weekend was incomplete if they didn't have the opportunity to enjoy pizza with "Uncle Stan" and his family. I never quite knew why they insisted on calling Stan their uncle, but I do know they loved him deeply.

The four boys were very close in age, but our son Eric was the oldest and usually insisted on being in charge. One hot summer afternoon the four boys were playing in a very small plastic pool in the backyard. We heard a loud scream! Seth, next in age to Eric, decided it was time to challenge Eric. He had found a pair of pliers, walked behind Eric, and clamped down on a chunk of bare skin on his back. Seth was little but quite strong for his age. Eric was screaming as if he were under attack by a grizzly bear. Stan ran into the backyard, grabbed the pliers from Seth, and rescued Eric. Believe it or not, the boys remained the best of friends!

Stan and I were forever on a diet. I remember him quipping on one occasion, "I've lost a thousand pounds in my lifetime, but it's always been the same ten pounds over and over!" Once Winnie and Linda decided to join Stan and me on a special diet. I don't recall the name of it, but I do remember that lunch consisted of one slice of cheese. We had been on the diet several days when Stan asked me to go with him to Columbus to visit parishioners who were hospitalized. We thought we were about to starve, so we convinced ourselves of the wisdom of having pizza for lunch at Stan's favorite pizza place, in the section of Columbus where Stan had grown up.

When we entered the restaurant, I placed my jacket onto a hook near our table. In one pocket of the jacket I had placed Stan's business card with his name, the name of his church, and all his contact information. Stan had given me the card when we entered the hospital a couple of hours before. He wanted me to have it in case anyone in the hospital questioned my being there.

We ate pizza until we were stuffed. We chuckled about the fact that Winnie and Linda were home suffering with only a slice of cheese for lunch. When we departed the restaurant, I absentmindedly left my jacket behind. We were so pleased with our accomplishment. When my coconspirator and I arrived at the parsonage in Washington Court House, we entered the house wearing big smiles. Our smiles quickly disappeared when the ladies in unison exclaimed, "So—how was your pizza?"

Yes, you guessed it. The waitress noticed that I had left my jacket behind, found Stan's card in the pocket of the jacket, and called the parsonage. When Linda answered, the waitress revealed our little secret. The next few days in the "doghouse" were not pleasant at all.

A quite bizarre incident occurred one chilly October evening in Ohio. Winnie and I and our three children had attended the Pumpkin Show in Circleville that night. The Pumpkin Show, often called "the greatest free show on earth," attracted hundreds of thousands of visitors each October. We had hurried home from the show because our favorite baseball team, the Dodgers, was playing in the World Series. When we parked in the garage, all of us exited the car very quickly. No one thought to close the front door on the passenger side of the car.

When the baseball game ended, it was time for bed. I walked into the kitchen and noticed that we had left the door from the kitchen to garage ajar. When I glanced into the garage, I noticed the open car door, so I dashed into the garage and closed it. It was late, and all of us were very tired. No one had noticed that our little poodle dog, Pixie, was missing.

The next morning after breakfast Winnie needed to drive into Circleville to buy some groceries. When she went into the garage and opened the car door, she screamed loudly! The entire family ran to the garage to see if Mom was in danger. About that time Pixie ran into the kitchen from the garage. Winnie stood frozen, looking into the car and explaining that Pixie had apparently been locked in the car all night. By this time all of us were peering into the car. We could see the damage clearly. The little dog, entrapped all night in the car in the dark garage, had fought hard to gain her freedom. She had eaten through the seat belt and with claws and teeth had removed all the plastic and form rubber that had covered the dash. It was stripped down to the metal. All the covering on the passenger-side door had been destroyed. Leather, cloth, and plastic were piled into the front seat. The front part of the car appeared to have been hit by nothing less than a tornado!

Our almost totally new car—the first new one we had owned in many years—appeared to have been destroyed. I immediately thought of the cost of repairs. It was especially troubling when I convinced myself that the insurance company would likely refuse to cover such damage. We prayed fervently for mercy as I dialed the phone to call Larry Plum, our insurance agent. He chuckled as I shared the story, but there was nothing funny at all in the moment. My concern turned to relief when Larry assured me that the damage would be fully covered. He then told me several similar stories of even greater damage done to vehicles by pets. This was in the early 1980s—can you believe the repairs cost over $2,500?

Winnie and I will always be grateful that Angie, Eric, and Jason spent some of their early school years in the Logan Elm School District, where their lives were enriched by some excellent teachers and administrators. Perhaps that is at least one reason that today Angie is an elementary school principal and Jason an elementary school teacher. Eric developed a keen appetite for learning, which was clearly a factor in his academic excellence, which laid the foundation for him to become a medical doctor.

It was during our years in Circleville that I received word that my Mom was nearing the end of her earthly journey. Winnie's dad had gone to heaven in 1980, the year we moved to Circleville. In 1984, in her eightieth year, my godly mother was largely confined to her bed and recliner. When I received the call that she was in the hospital and near the crossing into the celestial city of God, I hurried to be at her side and to express my heartfelt gratitude to this special woman of God, who had been mom and dad to me during my crucially important teenage years. She had worked long hours to provide for my sister and me and invested many hours praying for my salvation. She had always been the perfect example of Christlikeness. Furthermore, I wanted to once again thank her for the beautiful way she had welcomed Winnie into our family and for the love she had lavished upon Winnie. That Winnie and Mom were the closest of friends is one of the special joys of my life.

Not many hours after I expressed my love and appreciation to Mom, she quietly slipped away to be with Jesus, her Savior and Lord, whom she had faithfully served for many years. Both Winnie and I are so blessed to have had moms who loved us unconditionally.

On the day of my mother's funeral, hundreds gathered to pay tribute and to celebrate her Christlike life. Native American men and women telephoned to express their gratitude for the love she had shown them during the years she served as a volunteer missionary at Southwest Indian School in Arizona. Countless individuals talked with me at the funeral, reminding me that it was my mom who first invited them to church or first introduced them to Christ. Dozens recalled the countless times my mom transported them to Sunday School and church in her aging white Ford car.

I will never forget my mom's annual vegetable garden. She insisted that I plant and cultivate the garden filled with an abundance of most every vegetable that is delicious to eat. Every Saturday morning she would instruct me to harvest a generous supply of veggies that she could deliver to the homes of many of our neighbors. As she delivered the free vegetables with a big smile, she asked the parents if their children could go to Sunday School and church with her the next day. How could they say no as she handed them an abundant supply of great vegetables?

It was not unusual for her to transport fifty children to Sunday School each week. Of course, she had to make several trips to provide rides for everyone. Many of those riders were among those paying tribute to my mom after her death. They became leaders in our church and community.

During my years leading Circleville Bible College I received numerous invitations to speak in churches, missions conferences, and camp meetings. I mentioned earlier the impact of Taylor County Camp Meeting on my life and ministry. Gaskin Springs, Indian Springs, Avon Park, Multnomah, Sharon Center, Sebring, Lakeland, Camp Sychar, Stoutsville, Beulah, Frost Bridge and Mount of Praise are only a few of the camp meetings where I have had the joy of preaching the glorious gospel of our Lord Jesus.

At one of the camp meetings in Florida I heard the following story. I leave it with you to decide if it was only a tall tale.

It seems a man whose wife died in the Midwest moved to Florida, where he met a widow. He was 93, she was 88, and they fell in love! He asked her to marry him, and she agreed, so they set the date for their wedding.

Then a problem developed: he started experiencing memory loss. It seemed to be only partial—he could remember that he had asked her to marry him, but he could not recall her answer. After days of agonizing over the situation, he telephoned her to explain his dilemma. Haltingly and with considerable embarrassment, he explained that he recalled asking her to marry him but could not remember her answer.

She replied, "I'm so glad you called. I knew I had said yes to someone, but I couldn't remember who it was!"

Etched forever in my mind is my flight homeward after speaking in revival services in North Carolina. The date was April 14, 1988. I was aboard Piedmont Airlines flight 486 from

Charlotte, North Carolina, bound for Columbus, Ohio, when suddenly there was a very loud explosion as we were cruising along at 31,000 feet above West Virginia. The explosion destroyed one engine of the Fokker F28 jet and ripped a huge hole in the aircraft near the galley. We lost cabin pressure and plunged downward, seemingly destined to die in a fiery crash on a West Virginia mountainside. The captain's voice brought little hope when he announced that he would try to land the damaged aircraft at the Charleston, West Virginia, airport. His request for prayer was hardly necessary. To our amazement and great celebration, the landing was quite smooth. Looking at the broken hydraulic lines dangling in the gaping hole, I marveled that the pilot could control the badly damaged aircraft during the landing maneuvers.

Several days following this emergency landing, I received a letter from a lady in Alabama who years before had been a volunteer teacher at Southwest Indian School. She wrote,

> *I just wanted you to know that I prayed especially for you on April 14. I was working in my flower garden when God burdened me with an overwhelming sense of urgency to pray for your safety. I hurried to my bedroom and fell on my knees. I cried out to the Lord, "O God, Doug Carter is in danger. Please stretch forth Your mighty hand, place it beneath him, and keep him safe wherever he may be today." It was at 10:00 o'clock in the morning when I was interceding for you.*

Yes, she was praying at the exact time of the explosion. Would God have spared my life if she had failed to pray? I can't be certain, but I do know that God does many things only in answer to the prayers of His children.

The airplane incident was certainly not my first close call in a situation that could have resulted in serious injury or even death. Once during my preschool years I accidentally swallowed a nickel. It lodged in my windpipe and almost completely shut off my breathing. The local doctors could not remove it, so I was rushed to a large hospital in Augusta, where the doctors there were able to remove the coin and save my life.

In 1970 Winnie and I, along with two-year-old Angie, were traveling on an icy highway in near-blizzard conditions in western Oregon. The vehicle in front of us began spinning wildly like a top in the middle of the road as the driver apparently found it impossible to brake on the sheet of ice. As the vehicle finally came to a stop, our car rolled to a stop about two inches from an almost-certain collision.

On another occasion I was traveling alone on Interstate 10 headed south from Phoenix toward Tucson. Suddenly a tractor-trailer rig cut sharply and quickly into my lane. I had no choice but to depress the brakes as forcefully as possible and lost total control of my car as it began spinning on the freeway. Upon stopping, it rested upright in the middle of the road as a large truck and other vehicles were skidding to a stop just in time to avoid hitting my car!

Then there was the time in a small town in northwest Ohio when I fell asleep at the wheel in the wee hours of the morning. A lady who had stopped her car to use a pay phone saw all that happened as I drifted from my lane into the opposite lane and over against the curb on the wrong side of the street, where my car rolled to a stop. The woman came over, tapped on the driver's side window, and asked if I was okay. When I explained that I must have fallen asleep, she told me what she had observed. I think she believed my story—that I had preached at a church in Indiana and was driving back to my home in Ohio—when she noticed my Bible and sermon notes beside me on the front seat. Otherwise she just might have called the police.

I thank God for His protection on all these occasions. I'm inclined to think He has protected me countless other times when I did not even realize I was facing danger. And I'm sure that again and again God's faithful prayer warriors have been lifting me in prayer at the very times of my urgent needs.

Taylor County Camp Meeting, Butler, Georgia

In the summer of 1988 Winnie and I visited the Taylor County Camp Meeting at the invitation of Don Rollings, camp president, and George Luce, camp secretary.

Don had followed my mentor and hero, Rev. M. J. Wood, to the presidency when Brother Wood began experiencing declining health. Interestingly, Don was the person singing "The Love of God" during the Saturday morning service at Taylor County thirty years before when I committed my life to Christ.

When we arrived at the camp meeting, Don and George stated that they felt very strongly that I should become the next president of the camp. Don, who was not in good health at the time, stated that Brother Wood was in full agreement with him and George that I should serve as the next president, only the third in the history of the camp. Winnie and I agreed, somewhat reluctantly, that I would at least meet with the camp board to discuss possibilities. We questioned the wisdom of trying to lead a camp meeting in Georgia while residing in the Midwest.

The rest is now history. I couldn't say "no" to serving this place that had played such a pivotal role in Winnie's and my spiritual life. From 1989 through 2013 Winnie and I traveled every summer to this rustic facility in rural Georgia and found it always a refreshing, renewing spiritual oasis on the journey of life. The music, the preaching, the rich fellowship with godly men and women, the delicious meals, the lives of children, youth, and adults transformed by the power of the gospel, plus missionaries sent to the ends of the earth will never be forgotten. We'll gladly forget the spiders, snakes, and countless hours of hard work in the heat and humidity of July in central Georgia.

Interestingly, when I accepted the presidency at Taylor County Camp Meeting, I anticipated that Pastor Wood, Don, and George would have several years to stand by my side. However, within the first year of my presidency both Brother Wood and George were promoted to heaven, and Don was in declining health.

I was traveling when word came of Brother Wood's promotion to his heavenly home. I was heartbroken that I was unable to accept the invitation to share a tribute at his funeral service. I did send a letter that Brother Luce read at the service. The following paragraphs are from that letter:

> *Words are woefully inadequate to express my love for Brother Wood. He believed in me! He saw possibilities in a very shy, bashful country lad who was left without a father at age eleven. He taught me to love the Word of God, and he led me to embrace God's sanctifying grace, resulting in the reality of a pure heart and a Spirit-led life. He confronted me with the needs of a lost world. He dared me to follow Christ at any cost.*
>
> *Brother Wood was the most courageous Christian soldier I have ever known, and I am determined to "fight on" until that day when King Jesus returns in power and great glory and I am privileged to join with Brother Wood in an eternal celebration of God's grace and salvation! Brother Wood's name is surely enshrined forever in God's Hall of Fame! His memory will ever challenge and inspire me to love the Word, preach the truth, endeavor to rescue the perishing, and help to spread the glorious gospel of our Lord Jesus to the ends of the earth.*

We rejoice that we've had the joy of knowing and loving some of God's choice people because of our affiliation with Taylor County Camp Meeting: Franklin and Bernice Mc-Cants; Laurence Luce Sr. and his wife, Helen; their sons, George, Buddy, and Joe and their families; Jim and Elizabeth Browning; Ray Brockinton; Marvin Peed; Lester Peed; Bobby and Elaine Peed; Wayne and Marcia Templeton; Alan Wood and his family; Carey and Susan Peed; Fred and Mary Ellen Gardner; Frank and Millie Ziegler; Bill and Betsy Tarr; Terry and Minda McCants; Richie and Lynne McCants; Don and Jean Rollings; Lee and Paula Crist; Melvin and Janis Whitley; Gregg and Margaret Arnold; Roger and Joy Hencley; Bill and Hazel Branton; Tex and Wanda Watson; Elroy and Janice Douglas; Danny and Lori Peed; Henry and Nell Askew; Betty Clark; and Donnelle Wright and her kitchen crew—these are just a few of the hundreds who have added so much blessing and value to our lives.

The visiting evangelists, Bible teachers, and musicians profoundly and powerfully touched and enriched our lives. We were privileged to hear the very best!

World Gospel Mission, Marion, Indiana

In the spring of 1989 Tom Hermiz, president of World Gospel Mission, asked me to meet him for breakfast at Bob Evans restaurant in Circleville. There he invited me to join the administrative team at WGM as the vice president in charge of field ministries. Both Winnie and I loved WGM and had always felt we would return to missionary service. After several days of prayer, we felt Tom's invitation was God's way of releasing us at Circleville Bible College and placing us in a key role to serve missionaries around the world. We accepted the call and made plans to move to Indiana in the summer of 1989.

The move was not easy for the children. Angie was about to begin her senior year at the college, Eric would start high school in the fall, and Jason was entering the sixth grade. Jason, who values friendships about as much as any person on the planet, found it extremely difficult to leave his friends. But God has His way of taking care of His children. Interestingly, Angie would complete her studies at Circleville and later move to Indiana, where she would earn her teaching credentials at Indiana Wesleyan University and land her first teaching job in Marion. Eric would graduate as valedictorian of his high school.

In the spring of 1993 the Indiana Civil Liberties Union sent letters to all school systems in Indiana stating that prayer at graduation "is forbidden by the Establishment Clause of the First Amendment." Lawsuits were threatened against school systems that violated that regulation. The senior class of Mississinewa High School in Gas City voted to have prayer at their graduation despite the warnings from the ICLU. The *Twin City Journal-Reporter* of Gas City in their edition of May 28, 1993, wrote—

Eric Carter, who will be giving the valedictorian address, said he believes prayer should be a part of the graduation. At past graduation ceremonies there has been a scheduled Scripture reading. There is, however, no Scripture reading scheduled for this year's ceremony, so Carter said he intends to incorporate text from the Bible into his speech.

Eric completed his undergraduate degree at Ball State University in three years with a perfect 4.00 grade-point average and graduated from Indiana University School of Medicine. Jason later graduated from Indiana Wesleyan and still lives in Marion, where he is a teacher— and he is still surrounded by scores of friends. Angie's daughter, Shelby, our first grandchild, was born in Marion in 2000.

When we moved to Indiana we purchased a home in Gas City, a community located in Grant County near Marion. I have always believed that Christians should be actively involved in the life of their local communities, that this is a vital part of our being "salt and light," as Jesus instructed. In addition to being active in our church in Gas City, I participated in civic organizations in Marion and Gas City. Similarly, while we lived in Ohio I was very active in the Circleville-Pickaway County community through civic organizations, the chamber of commerce, and the local school district.

Several years after our move to Indiana, several local friends began encouraging me to seek political office. Even I was greatly surprised when I felt the Lord leading me to run for a seat on the city council in Gas City. I was quite sure that an outsider and relative stranger to the community could never get elected, but I knew obedience to the Lord was my only acceptable option. I was elected by a few percentage points over a popular incumbent but was reelected four years later by a huge majority. The position on the council gave me a platform to speak out on several key moral issues.

It doesn't bother me when pastors refuse to endorse candidates or political parties, but I'm appalled at the silence of so many Christian leaders, especially pastors, on the great moral issues confronting society. As examples, how can we cowardly stick our heads in the sand as millions of babies are slaughtered and biblical marriage is redefined?

As I think back to my childhood, I recall that my dad often talked with me about politics. Even back in the 1940s he would comment about the growing size and power of the federal bureaucracy. He often warned that a government big enough to give us anything we want would also be powerful enough to take everything we have. He avidly listened every evening to the news on radio. I can still see him seated beside his Philco radio as he listened to a series of fifteen-minute programs featuring famous newsmen of his day, H. V. Kaltenborn, Lowell Thomas, Edward R. Murrow, Paul Harvey, Fulton Lewis Jr., and Gabriel Heatter. I would often sit beside him and listen to these superb communicators. Perhaps this is why I have always had a special interest in history, current events, politics, and global issues. Dad was a Christian, a conservative, and a Republican—in that order!

Burnis Bushong, who was retiring after many years as the vice president of field ministries at World Gospel Mission, invited me to travel around the world with him in the spring of 1989. A walking encyclopedia of knowledge about world missions, he had been a key mentor in my life for many years. I was so blessed that he invited me on this trip, where he introduced me to so many missionaries I would soon be serving and leading. Even though I had done some international travel previously, it was this trip that instilled in my heart a passion to invest my life in serving missionaries and national pastors. Little did I know that over the next twenty-five years I would travel to one hundred fourteen nations, visiting many of them numerous times. Winnie has often traveled with me and has even put together a list of the most beautiful places she has visited: Edinburgh, Scotland; Tiberius, Israel; Zermatt, Switzerland; and the "tea country" near Kericho, Kenya.

There were many memorable trips. I visited Kenya and Tanzania with Tom Hermiz and Tim Hawk; Burundi and India with Stan Lewis; and Bolivia, Paraguay, and Argentina with David Kushman. It was on a trip to South America that I mistakenly wore shoes that did not match. I made the discovery in the airport in Miami—too late to correct the situation!

In Kenya I waited alone under a tree at one end of the landing strip in the Maasai tribal region, awaiting a small, single-engine aircraft to pick me up for my flight to Nairobi. As I waited I heard noise in the distance. Peering toward the noise, I saw a herd of cattle accompanied by several tall, thin Maasai warriors with spears and clubs moving directly toward me. While I didn't feel completely safe, I saw no place to hide, so I simply waited for them. One of them walked up to me and began touching the hairs on my arms and my chest. He turned to his friends and grinned, then pulled back the red cloth in which he was wrapped. I believe he wanted to show me that he had no hairs on his chest. Whatever the reason, he giggled loudly, motioned to his friends, and ran down the path behind the cows.

On my initial trip to Japan with Dr. Bushong in 1989 I was quite intrigued by a special moment at a Bible college near Tokyo. After the graduates received their diplomas, they returned to their seats, where they stood facing the headmaster of the college and the top official of their denomination. The official then, one by one, called the name of a male graduate and a female graduate, announcing that this couple would soon become husband and wife and would be assigned to serve a specific church or mission field. For each couple, when the announcement was made, the two graduates bowed their heads and graciously affirmed their acceptance of the marriage plans and the ministry assignment. This continued until all graduates were informed of their mates and ministry locations. No one objected.

I learned later that the graduates had studied four years with no dating permitted. The school officials had carefully observed each student throughout the four years and made note of his or her personality, talents, and spiritual gifts. After much thought and prayer, the leaders met to decide to whom each graduate would be married and where he or she would be placed in ministry. I also learned that all students had officially agreed to this process when enrolling as freshmen. Another official commented that there had been no divorces, adding, "They marry and then fall in love."

On one of my many trips to Kenya, I asked the head of the Africa Gospel Church if he could give me a list of the qualities he would love to see in a missionary sent to his nation. After sharing a couple of items, he paused for a moment and said, "Please, just send us missionaries like Ernie Steury." Because of my friendship with Ernie and awareness of his humility and lifetime of sacrificial service as a medical doctor in Kenya, I needed no further explanation. When Jesus is shared by our words and seen in our lives, there will always be major impact upon others.

One memorable evening in Kenya, Winnie and I were guests for dinner in the home of O. E. and Mariam Joseph, a lovely couple from India serving as missionaries with WGM in Kenya. The meal was Mexican. Yes, here we were, Americans visiting in Kenya and enjoying a delicious Mexican meal prepared by our Indian friends.

My international travels were keeping me away from home during a crucially important time in the lives of Eric and Jason. They did not want me missing their athletic events, and

I certainly didn't want to miss their games. When I shared my concern with Dr. Hermiz, he stated that he had been thinking about beginning a new department of advancement at WGM and asking me to direct it. I was overjoyed. While I enjoyed overseas travel and loved my interaction with missionaries and national leaders, I truly needed to be closer to home for a few years. Furthermore, I have always loved asking God's people to invest His resources into His goals and objectives on earth. I was firmly convinced that raising funds if done God's way is about raising His people to be more like Jesus, that generosity is the intersection that connects the Great Commandment with the Great Commission.

In addition to international travel to serve missionaries and national leaders, I frequently spoke in churches, camp meetings, and conferences. In October 1996 while in southern Indiana to preach revival services, I was asked by a friend to go with him to visit a twenty-five-year-old quadriplegic. The young man had suffered paralysis from the neck down in a terrible automobile accident eight years before. When I walked into the living room and saw the young man sitting motionless in this motorized wheelchair, I could hardly believe that he was once a high school star football running back who could dash forty yards in four and a half seconds.

After greeting me, he began telling me that Jesus had forgiven his sins and transformed his life. With a smile he commented, "I'm so richly blessed and so thankful for God's wonderful grace. When I was strong and could run like the wind, I was self-centered, self-sufficient, and didn't know God, but the accident brought me face to face with my need for God. The old Nick is gone—I'm now a new creation in Christ. He fills my heart with joy."

With the radiant joy of Christ shining from his face, he explained, "I'll walk again someday, maybe in this life—but certainly in the next!" In my mind I could see him leaping down the streets of gold in the New Jerusalem. There are no wheelchairs in heaven.

Then he made a statement I'll never forget. Speaking slowly but with certainty, he said, "If walking again in this life would lead me to be self-sufficient again and cause me to drift away from God, then I'd earnestly pray that He would leave me as I am. I have peace and joy in my heart, the Holy Spirit to comfort and guide me, and the promise of eternity with my Savior—so really, how could I ask for more?"

As I left his room that day, I knew I had witnessed a far greater miracle than physical healing. I had seen a young man living victoriously in the middle of what looked like a tragedy. I had seen an individual who focused on God, not on his circumstances. I had witnessed a believer accepting a situation that will not make sense until the day when we see circumstances in reverse. I had seen faith embracing God's promises with such resolve that it could relinquish present questions for the sake of future answers.

I went back to my room later that day and began writing down my thoughts about my meeting with Nick. My written notes that day became the beginning of a book I would eventually title *Big Picture People*. This little book, published in 2000 by Beacon Hill Press of Kansas City, has been used by the Holy Spirit to help countless individuals see God faithfully at work in their lives, even in the midst of the most difficult of circumstances.

I have enjoyed the support of very gifted administrative assistants. Three of them ended up in full-time missionary service: Bev Cordell Donahue assisted me at Circleville Bible College, and Rebecca Higgins and Cathleen Strong at World Gospel Mission headquarters. When I set up the advancement office at WGM, Bonnie Kellogg ably served as my executive assistant. The addition of Dan Schafer to the advancement team greatly enhanced the impact of the department.

Winnie worked in the accounting department at WGM. Both of us cherish many special memories of our years working closely with the WGM staff, missionaries, board members, and donors. We are better people and Christian servants because our lives have been touched by George and Bertha Warner, Hollis and Ruby Abbott, Ray and Maralyn Lyne, Jimmy and Kitty Lentz, Dale and Glenna Dorothy, Tom and Ella Mae Hermiz, Burnis and Thelma Bushong, Denis and Mary Applebee, John and Mabel Kunkle, Billy Wayne and Jenny Fuller, Jon and Lisa Mayo, Tim and Sharon Hawk, Dan and Pam Schafer, Bob and Peggy Bushong, Don and Twana Hawk, Dennis and Twana Johnson, Gene and Marion Lewton, Ernie and Sue Steury, Meredythe Schefflin, Stan and Carolyn Lewis, Noritta

Carter, Phil and June Simms, David and Christie Engbrecht, Roy and Sue Lauter, Bob and Bonnie Hudson, Mel and Sally Truex, Bobby and Elaine Peed, Kay Young, Leona Taves, and Lee and Paula Crist, to name only a few of hundreds we hold dear to our hearts.

While so many have added immense value and blessing to our lives, I am especially grateful for those who played key mentoring roles in my growth as a Christ-follower and leader. My mom was a beautiful example of Christlikeness. Pastor M. J. Wood taught me to love the Word of God and to build a biblical foundation for my life and ministry. Jimmy Lentz modeled effective communication skills, Burnis Bushong stretched my heart to embrace the whole world, Stan Toler helped take my people skills and attitude tenacity to a much higher level, and Ray Lyne shared insights that changed fundraising into joyful spiritual ministry that was truly transformational for many who embraced the principles of biblical stewardship and generosity. My wife Winnie's heart of selflessness and attitude of gratitude overflows daily in a lifestyle of generosity that challenges and inspires me. From John Maxwell I learned leaders' math— strategic thinking, the power of partnership, and compound results.

I'll never forget Stan Toler's contagious smile, positive attitude, and spirit of generosity. He stared a story with me that I've told countless times around the world, although he never claimed it was true.

He said that a wealthy Texan decided to have a contest on his huge ranch in west Texas. He sent notices about the contest to all the handsome young bachelors in his area inviting them to compete for one of three prizes: a thousand acres of his best land, the hand of his beautiful daughter in marriage, or a million dollars.

Young men came from everywhere on the designated Saturday morning. He lined them up at the end of his Olympic-size swimming pool and explained that the contestants would be expected to swim from one end of the pool to the other end. The first one out of the pool at the other end would be the winner. He lifted his pistol to fire the shot to begin the race.

Then he paused a moment and said, "Before I fire the shot, you need to know that this pool is filled with wall-to-wall death. I have traveled the world and collected every kind of deadly water monster I could find. They are all in this pool."

The gun sounded and only one man jumped into the pool. He emerged quickly from the opposite end of the pool, spitting, sputtering, wiping water from his face, and brushing hair from his eyes. As the brave young bachelor ran toward the rancher, the rancher exclaimed, "Congratulations, young man. Now, which do you want—a thousand acres of my best land, my beautiful daughter's hand in marriage, or a million dollars?"

The young man shouted, "I don't want any of them—I just want to know who pushed me in!"

Other than my mother, who beautifully modeled Christlike living, it was Brother Wood who most impacted me by helping me build a solid biblical foundation for my life and ministry. While he was an avid reader and admired many authors, he was truly a man of *one* book—the Holy Bible—and helped me grasp the big story of the Word of God. The Bible discloses the holy and gracious heart of God, exposes the sinful heart of humankind, and proposes God's remedy for sin—forgiveness of sinful conduct and cleansing of the sinful nature.

He also helped me see the big *picture* painted by the Word of God. The Old Testament declares that Jesus the Messiah-Redeemer is coming! The gospels proclaim that He has come to pay the price for our salvation! Acts to Revelation explains that He has returned to the Father and sent His Spirit to indwell His followers and one day is coming again!

EQUIP Leadership, Atlanta, Georgia

In the summer of 1996 I received one of the most significant phone calls of my life. I was preparing to drive from Indiana to Ohio to speak at historic Camp Sychar when my assistant announced that John Maxwell was on the line. It had been my joy to know John since I was the visiting missionary speaker in his church in Lancaster, Ohio, in 1976. His dad had become one of my spiritual heroes. I was well aware that God had wonderfully blessed John's ministry at Skyline Wesleyan Church in San Diego and had begun opening doors for him to teach leadership to many pastors and marketplace leaders and to speak to huge audiences in numerous locations. I knew his books were becoming increasingly popular. His brother, Larry, who served on the WGM board, had become a special friend I so greatly admired for his business expertise and generosity in support of God's work.

But quite frankly, I had no idea why John would be calling me. I surely did not know that this phone call would change the course of my life and provide an opportunity to have impact in all the nations of the world.

John said, "Doug, I want you to take a trip with me."

"Where are we going?"

"Not where you think." I sat down. He added, "I believe the greatest need today around the world is for more and better Christian leaders."

He went on to explain how God had placed in his heart a vision to train, resource, and encourage Christian leaders in every nation. The vision was clear and compelling. Instantly I wanted to become a part of this, but I restrained my excitement. John explained that a great vision without a great team is a nightmare. I asked him to tell me about the team he had put together for the new ministry he was calling "EQUIP."

He replied, "Well, Doug, when you join the team, it will have one member!"

Winnie and I didn't need to pray long before we knew God was directing us to embrace wholeheartedly this dream that God had birthed in the heart of John Maxwell. We flew down to Springdale, Arkansas, to meet with John and Larry Maxwell to learn more about EQUIP and to discuss the role I could play on the team. Before the meeting ended, a handshake and a hug sealed the deal. Winnie and I would move to Atlanta in the spring of 1997 and become a part of the interesting, exciting, and life-changing world of John Maxwell. Little did we realize that John and Larry had just offered us a platform from which we could touch every nation!

Even though Winnie and I were certain that God was leading us to Atlanta, the day we drove away from our house in Gas City leaving all three of our children behind in Indiana was one of the most painful of our lives.

I officially began with EQUIP December 1, 1996, but the opening of the offices of INJOY, INJOY Stewardship Services, and EQUIP in the Atlanta area wouldn't happen until early summer 1997. In 1997 Tim Elmore, Dennis Worden, Linda Kirk, Ron McManus, and a few others became members of the EQUIP team.

Ron McManus, our founding president, arranged for John Maxwell, Tim Elmore, and me to join him in teaching leadership in India in September 1997. I plunged into my role of asking God's people to invest financially in the EQUIP vision while Tim Elmore focused on developing leadership curriculum. Generous gifts from Jim and Nancy Dornan, Tom and Joan Philippe, Larry and Anita Maxwell, Ray and Tami Moats, Gerald and Geni Brooks, Don and Doris Meyer, Alton Garrison and his church in North Little Rock, and others played a key role in getting EQUIP successfully off the launch pad.

Don Meyer was the first person I contacted about a gift to EQUIP. We had no track record of success and no stories I could share with Don, just a vision that burned in our hearts to walk beside leaders worldwide adding value to them and helping them move from addition to multiplication in ministry results. Don believed in the vision. He gave us $25,000—the first dollars of millions that God would help us raise for the sole purpose of developing effective Christian leaders around the world.

God wonderfully blessed the leadership conferences in India in the fall of 1997. Approximately ten thousand pastors attended training in five cities of India. Even though we were there teaching, we were also listening. It was obvious from the start that God had raised up EQUIP to respond to the cry from leaders around the world for biblical servant leadership training. With the Great Commission as our mandate and the leadership training methods of Jesus as our inspiration, John Maxwell and the EQUIP leadership team served leaders in the Philippines, Indonesia, Hong Kong, and Singapore. Additionally, we were striving to serve college and university students in America as well as pastors serving churches in the largest urban centers of our nation.

Traveling with John Maxwell is always a quite an adventure. I will always thank God for the many trips I made with him in the United States and to many other nations. I recall vividly a special moment on our first trip to India. John and I had just boarded a small twin-engine, propeller-type aircraft when the pilot attempted to start the engines. One engine started immediately, but the other had not started after a long wait. Someone, perhaps a maintenance man, left the cockpit and went outside and began banging on the faulty engine with a sledgehammer. After he had pounded on it at least a dozen times, John turned to me and said, "If that man returns to the aircraft to fly with us, we'll remain on board—but if he doesn't return, we'll get off this plane one way or the other."

After the man beat on the engine a few more times, the propeller began turning. He returned to the airplane, and we took off for our conference in Kota, India, where the Holy Spirit powerfully ministered to over 2,000 pastors gathered there. Those pastors have since planted tens of thousands of churches across the nation.

John Maxwell is a master of one-liners, brief statements loaded with meaning. He has uttered thousands of them, such as the following:

> *Leaders are developed daily, not in a day.*
> *Pay now; play later.*
> *Leaders know the way, go the way, and show*
> *the way.*
> *When we develop leaders, multiplication—*
> *not addition—is always the result.*

I have spoken a few of my own one-liners:

> *Discipline yourself and no one else will*
> *ever need to.*
> *Some people bring joy when they arrive;*
> *others bring joy when they leave.*

*Many people serve things and use God; a few
serve God and use things.
God may ask many things from you in your
lifetime, but advice is not one of them.*

There's never a dull moment when traveling with John. One afternoon when I was with him in Manila for his scheduled talk with the National Police Academy, a group of policemen on motorcycles came to our hotel several hours before the event and explained that they would be escorting us to the academy.

Traffic jams greeted us in many nations, and it was the same here in the Philippines. The late afternoon traffic was terrible. After moving very slowly for about an hour, the traffic came to a complete stop. Slowly the motorcycle patrol cleared the way for us to cross the median and begin moving in the opposite direction of the six lanes of oncoming traffic. We inched along as the patrol divided the six lanes right down the middle to make way for our caravan. Even with a police escort, we arrived two hours late for John to speak to the top law enforcement officials in the nation. We chuckled about it, but they appeared quite embarrassed.

Tim Elmore and I had the privilege of traveling to the Middle East in 1998 to lay the groundwork for EQUIP to begin training in Lebanon and Egypt. Eventually leaders from twenty-two nations of the region would receive Christ-centered leadership training in Beirut, Cairo, and Amman (Jordan).

Not long ago I received a letter from a pastor in the Middle East who had attended several of the leadership conferences that Tim and I taught in Beirut in the early years of EQUIP. The following is an excerpt from that letter:

I am writing to say thanks to John Maxwell, Doug Carter, the EQUIP staff, donors, and associate trainers who have invested in my life for almost twenty years. When I attended the first EQUIP conference in Beirut, Doug Carter and Tim Elmore were the teachers. As they taught biblical leadership principles, I immediately made a shocking discovery—I was the problem at my church!

I had been leading a church in Jordan for twelve years, and it had been stuck at about sixty-five in attendance for all those years. As I listened to the lessons, I realized that I was the lid on my church. I had equipped no laity for ministry and trained no leaders to serve with me.

Equipped with training notebooks from EQUIP, I returned to my church committed to practice all I had learned. I apologized to my congregation for my terrible leadership and shared that I was learning a new model of leadership with Jesus as my example. I asked if others wanted to study and learn with me. Six people volunteered to begin the journey.

What has happened in my life and in my church since then is a miracle of God's grace and a testimony to the power of biblical leadership principles. Hundreds of leaders in Jordan and other nations have been trained through our church. Today we are a congregation of one thousand Jordanians with an additional six thousand Iraqi and Syrian refugees. We have planted churches in Jordan and four other nations of our region. We focus on evangelism, discipleship, and leadership training. During these very dark years in the Middle East multitudes are coming to Christ.

Many people have touched my life, but John Maxwell, Doug Carter, and the EQUIP team have made the investment that has made the greatest difference. Because of you, I embraced a huge vision from God and rejected those who argued that churches could not grow in our region.

Kevin Donaldson joined the EQUIP administrative team to oversee our growing network of conferences around the world. Sam Chand headed up the urban arena of ministry, and Tim Elmore focused on American students even as he developed international study guides.

September 11, 2001, changed the landscape for everyone. In the last quarter of 2001 our gift income diminished to only a trickle. John Hull, who had become our president in 2000, challenged us to spend our lunch hours in prayer and fasting.

John Maxwell and the board of directors decided that we need-ed to focus our limited resources solely on the international community. It was during this very difficult season that John asked, "What difference would it make if we could raise up one million effective Christian leaders around the world"?

The discussion that followed resulted in the launch of the Million Leaders Mandate in 2003 with its clear mission of training and resourcing one million Christian leaders world-wide, beginning in Asia and concluding in South America eight years later. India, the Philippines, and Indonesia came first. The training would be done by volunteer associate train-ers, pastors, and Christian business leaders, primarily North Americans, who would give generously of their dollars to print notebooks and pay their own travel expenses every six months for a period of three years to teach EQUIP leadership lessons to Christian leaders at a specific site. The very first conference was in Mumbai, India, with Mark Miller and Skip Ross serving as the trainers.

In subsequent years the Million Leaders Mandate was launched in the Middle East, Africa, Europe, Latin America, and China. John Maxwell and others of us on the EQUIP lead-ership team participated in the "launch trips." The associate trainers came behind and began the process of training leaders every six months. By 2006 the goal of one million leaders had been reached! But we *continued* training!

Tom Atema, one of our associate trainers in Beirut, Leba-non, was invited to join the EQUIP team primarily to build strategic partnerships with other international organizations. These ministries would provide personnel to train leaders in their streams of influence, and EQUIP would provide curriculum. Because of MLM and the global partnerships, EQUIP's influence quickly spread across the globe. Today EQUIP is serving leaders in one hundred eighty of the one hundred ninety-six nations, and a plan was in place to reach every nation by the end of 2015. We are also investing in leaders in many territories not officially recognized as independent nations.

In addition to my role as the chief development officer of EQUIP, I was asked to give guidance to EQUIP's strategy to raise up leaders in China. Following a China Summit in Midland, Texas, and subsequent meetings in Atlanta, John Maxwell and the leadership team at EQUIP decided to begin leadership training in China, the most populous nation of our planet. Because of the size of the nation and the complexity of ministry there, we agreed to a multi-layered strategy that would target the registered churches, the unregistered or underground church networks (commonly called house churches), the expatriate fellowship groups, and young urban professionals, including university students.

I felt the Holy Spirit prompting me to telephone Pastor Chris Hodges in Birmingham to share our vision and strategize with him. I shared that the project would cost several hundred thousand dollars to launch. I wept tears of joy when he replied that God had already spoken to him about China and that he and his church had already begun saving money for outreach there. He agreed to fund this huge initiative to invest in Christian leaders in this nation of well over a billion people.

We launched training in the registered churches and expatriate community in China in partnership with Beijing International Christian Fellowship. Our passion to serve the unregistered house churches in China became a reality through a partnership with a ministry well connected in China. Seven years ago Tim Elmore and I launched the training for the house church leaders. I have continued teaching the top leaders of the five largest networks and four of the smaller regional networks. These leaders oversee and care for tens of millions of believers in China. Over one million Chinese pastors have been trained. We have now completed three volumes of training in China. Because the government has intensified its persecution of Christians, the introduction of the new Salt & Light evangelism curriculum has been temporarily delayed.

As millions of Chinese have moved from the countryside into the massive urban areas, it has been so heartwarming to see well-trained leaders planting thousands of growing churches in the cities. Equally exciting is the passion of the Chinese church to become a mission force impacting all of Asia for Christ. This dream is beginning to become reality.

The top leader of each of the unregistered (house church) networks is affectionately referred to as "Uncle." I loved hearing the Uncles share their personal testimonies.

The senior leader of a national "house church" network has been preaching and starting churches in many provinces. He began thirty-three years ago at age seventeen. When he was thirteen his dad died. His mom, in his words, was demon possessed. In his town there were six elderly ladies who were believers, and none of them could read. They did not have a Bible but had the words to some hymns. They asked this young man to read the songs to them, and the words introduced him to Jesus.

He told the ladies that his mom was controlled by demons and asked the ladies to ask Jesus to heal her. The women came to his house and prayed for his mom. He wrote down the words to the prayers and often prayed these words for her. Eventually, one day she asked Jesus to save her, and she was set free! Because of her transformation, he believed as well. Their home became a house church, and he began writing hymns and preaching, walking all night to go to other villages to preach. When he finally got a bicycle, he would travel day and night by bike to go to other provinces to preach and start churches. In those days many people worshiped idols and were enslaved by evil spirits. Everywhere he preached people were set free. Thousands believed in Jesus.

Another Uncle shared that he came to Christ at age twelve and began preaching at age seventeen, going village to village to plant churches. From age seventeen to age sixty-three he was imprisoned seven times for a total of twenty-seven years. For the other nineteen years he planted thousands of churches. During one long period of confinement in a large prison with five thousand inmates, he led over four thousand to Christ.

Almost ten million Chinese believers now attend the network of "underground" churches that he leads.

This Uncle's story spans from Mao's regime to today. He faithfully served Christ even when targeted for prison, work camps, and torture. When he shared his testimony with me, he repeatedly mentioned the sacrifice of countless Christians who loved and served Jesus—regardless of the cost. He expressed that their obedience helped to reach millions for Christ and to ignite in the hearts of Chinese believers a vision and passion to reach not only China but also the entire world with the gospel.

It has been my joy to teach leadership in dozens of locations in China, often in nondescript, off-the-beaten-path hotels located in the suburbs of major cities. I have also taught in many of the unregistered churches that meet in a variety of facilities ranging from warehouses to apartments to conference rooms in office buildings to hotel conference rooms.

A few of these gatherings are forever etched in my mind. One Easter Sunday morning in a major city of China, Winnie and I attended a house church meeting in a conference room in a small hotel. After I preached the Easter message and concluded the time of prayer with seekers, I helped to baptize several converts in a bathtub in one of the hotel guest rooms. One of the ladies baptized, along with two of her adult daughters, had been previously employed by the Chinese government to head up the propaganda efforts to promote atheism throughout the nation.

Many of the leadership conferences were memorable. One evening I was transported by car from my hotel to a street corner where I was asked to leave the car and stand under a streetlight until another car came along offering me a ride. I was informed that the driver would call to me using a fictitious name.

After waiting for several minutes in the darkness except for the dimly lit streetlight, the second car approached and the driver called to me using my strange new name. I climbed into the backseat of the car. We drove for about an hour into a residential area of small homes surrounded by high fences. The driver motioned for me to keep my head down as he backed his car into an alley behind a row of houses. Someone opened the car door and motioned for me to follow. I noticed that several men lined my path on either side. I was hurried into the home through the back door and into a fairly small bedroom where at least fifty men and women were gathered.

At about 8:00 in the evening the host announced that the leadership training would begin. He informed the group that I would cover six leadership lessons over the next six hours and that we would take a coffee and tea break about midnight. He told me that all the attendees gathered in the room were key Christian leaders, several from western China, with some of them coming from Tibet. Every attendee listened intently to every word, even in the crowded and uncomfortable conditions. When I concluded the training in the early hours of the morning, they insisted on a time of questions and answers—like starving people who had found bread.

During many of my trips to China I also visited Singapore, Indonesia, the Philippines, Taiwan, Japan, South Korea, Malaysia, Cambodia, Vietnam, and other nations of the region. There were countless opportunities to teach leadership conferences and to engage in discussions with key Christian leaders in these nations. One evening in Singapore I met with a business leader from Hong Kong. After a long discussion of biblical leadership principles, he began sharing his personal testimony. For well over an hour I listened as he shared his faith story.

My new friend had grown up in Hong Kong. He first learned about Christ through a businessman from Australia when the two of them were traveling in Papua New Guinea, and he invited Christ into his heart. When he returned to Hong Kong, this Chinese man obtained a copy of the Bible and began reading it daily. As he studied the Word, grew deeper in his faith, and discovered biblical principles of stewardship, he concluded that God was the owner of his business. Motivated by a desire to make an eternal difference in the lives of others, he began giving generously to his local church and sharing his faith in the marketplace.

By the time he had reached middle age, he was highly successful in business. Challenged by his pastor to go with him to visit secretly with house church leaders in mainland China, he and his wife decided to make the journey. As he listened to house church leaders share stories of facing persecution each day for the sake of the gospel, he and his wife heard and obeyed the call of God to move to the mainland to invest their lives in serving house church pastors and their families.

After selling their business and their home, they moved to a remote area of China for the purpose of building a residential school to serve the children of house church families. They invested all their wealth in the construction and operation of this Christian high school, knowing full well that at any time the government could come and seize ownership of the school. Furthermore, they knew they could be imprisoned for teaching the Bible.

Indeed, one day officials from the central government came for the purpose of closing the school and seizing all the assets. My friend pleaded with the authorities to interview the students before making a final decision to close the school. As the officials talked with many of the students, they discovered that the students were very happy, cared deeply about others, loved their nation, and desired to make a positive difference with their lives. When the Communist officials met with my friend at the end of the day, they said, "The school will remain open"—and then asked, "When can we enroll our children here?"

Over the years the school has continued to lovingly and effectively serve the children of house church Christians. The school has also enrolled hundreds of children of government officials. Many of these young men and women have become followers of Christ and have led their parents to the Savior.

Several years after I began serving with EQUIP, I received word that my beloved Native American friend in Arizona, Erwin Patricio, had passed on to his heavenly home. His daughter, Maxine, telephoned to ask me to speak for his funeral. Only days before her call I had undergone major surgery and had been forbidden to travel for four weeks. I called my surgeon and begged him to let me fly to Arizona to speak at the funeral for my very dear friend. After I shared Erwin's story with my doctor, he reluctantly agreed for me to travel and speak if I didn't stand for an extended time. The celebration of the life and ministry of Erwin was to be held outdoors on a mountainside on the Tohono O'odham Indian Reservation in southern Arizona.

Hundreds gather on the mountainside under the desert sun, coming from several states and many reservations. There was a public address system for the speakers and singers; however, there were no chairs to be found. So I stood . . . and stood . . . and stood. It was a glorious experience! The Holy Spirit moved mightily, and tears flowed down many faces as scores of men and women expressed gratitude for Erwin's impact upon their lives. Many stated that it was Erwin who had introduced them to Jesus. One young man commented, "To us Native people he was our Billy Graham!" Think about it—from "reservation drunkard" to "Billy Graham"! Let us never forget the power of the gospel of Jesus Christ to transform a life.

It has been my joy to invite God's people to invest in His goals and objectives on Planet Earth. Faithful and generous biblical stewards have responded with millions upon millions of dollars to help spread the fame and glory of Jesus to the ends of the earth. Quite frankly, my goal has never been to raise money but to help raise people of faith to be more like Jesus. The giver is always more important than the gift. Christ is the ultimate giver. We are most like Him when we are giving generously, lovingly, and selflessly. I have always endeavored to build lasting friendships with faithful ministry partners and to provide them with opportunities to lay up treasures in heaven.

Having been involved in development ministry since 1964, I have been blessed to have met hundreds of very generous biblical givers. I've stated often that God has given me the privilege of fellowship with some of the most Christlike men and women on our planet.

In 2007 my book *Raising More than Money* was published by Thomas Nelson. Many Christian leaders graciously endorsed the book. My dear friend Larry Plum summarized the book as follows:

> *Doug Carter may have written the most important book ever on biblical giving. From the perceptions of what wealth is and how God wants us to use it; to practical, organized and inspirational advice on how to give; to the step-by-step program for raising more than money, this book covers it all.*

The final story in my book was about my mom and her generous heart:

> *She (my mom) brought up two children on very limited income, but she never failed to give more than ten percent of her income to the Lord. When*

*she retired, she became a self-supporting mission-
ary to Native Americans in Arizona, serving there
about ten years. She spent the final few years of her
life pretty much confined to her home in Alma following a debilitating stroke.*

*I remember telephoning her one morning not
long before her promotion to heaven. When I asked
about her condition, she replied, "My body is weak,
but I've never been more alive. I'm truly the most
blessed person on earth. This morning I read my
Bible, a love letter from my Father; then on the
wings of prayer I visited about twenty-five countries as I interceded for missionaries I love. Then
I wrote gift checks to my church, a mission agen-
cy, and a Christian college. Without leaving my
room, because of the wonderful privileges of prayer
and giving, today I have touched the face of God,
wrapped my arms around a lost world, and invested in the next generation of Christian leaders.
My heart overflows with joy!*

In early 2013 EQUIP began our new "hub," or regional
model, designed to train Christian leaders in the Middle East,
North Africa, and the Gulf states. It has been a rare and special
joy to work closely with Michel Khalil, our regional director
for the Middle East, in this new model. My burden to develop
a vanguard of transformational leaders in this region of the
world is longstanding. In addition to training in Beirut and

Cairo, I visited Iraq with John Hull shortly after Saddam Hussein was toppled from power and met some of the pastors who had served during his reign of terror.

Likewise, I traveled to Iran and learned firsthand of the brutality of the Iranian government and the Islamic clerics toward followers of Christ. My heart longs to see this region of the world transformed as hearts are set free from the power of Satan and the culture is liberated from the deadly grip of Islam.

I will never forget the testimonies by the pastors in Iraq. One brother who led a house church told about his imprisonment in a dungeon in Baghdad. He described the total darkness in the dungeon, then described the glorious light that flooded the cell when Jesus appeared to him. He explained that Jesus said, "Fear not. I brought down Nebuchadnezzar and I will bring down Saddam Hussein." This man commented, "I realized that though I had lost everything—my family, my home, my freedom—I still had Jesus, and He is always enough." He fled the prison shortly thereafter when bombs were dropped near the prison and forced the dungeon door open. His church has since reached hundreds with the gospel.

The trip to Iraq in February 2004 with John Hull, Pastor Randy Pope of Perimeter Church, and Phil Orazi, an executive at Chick-fil-A, was powerfully used of God to persuade me to invest a substantial portion of my time in serving the persecuted church around the world as long as God gives me health and strength to do so. The trip to Iraq was for the purpose of conducting a leadership training conference in Erbil in northern Iraq. I recall vividly the spiral landing as the pilot flew circle after circle directly over the Baghdad airport. The landing was safe but most unusual. I learned later that the spiral landing was designed to avoid sniper fire. On our trip from the airport to our hotel in Baghdad we encountered the first of dozens of military checkpoints we would undergo in Iraq.

Rany Ghaly, a young Egyptian brother and friend who served part-time with EQUIP, greeted us in Baghdad. Rany also worked part-time with Kasr el Dobara Church in Cairo, the largest evangelical church in the Middle East. Our training in Iraq would be done in partnership with this church and their team of workers located in Kurdistan. Rany had arranged for us to meet with all twelve of the evangelical pastors in Baghdad, a city of five million people! Their stories of persecution and suffering under the brutality of Saddam Hussein were heartbreaking. On the other hand, we were inspired by their stories of God's faithfulness to them as they served in this dark, difficult, dangerous place. I specifically recall the pastor who shared that he was imprisoned four months, his father five years, and his mother over a year. What was their crime? Hosting a prayer meeting in their home had cost them their freedom. All the other pastors told similar stories.

Interestingly, most of the pastors were familiar with EQUIP and shared stories of the impact of the curriculum upon their lives and ministries. They explained that pastors in Jordan had smuggled the EQUIP materials to them.

One pastor shared that he was in the military when he learned that his sister had become a Christian. He was outraged, went to the family home, and beat his sister unmercifully. He told her that he would beat her every week until she abandoned her faith in Christ. He searched until he found a Bible that he could read and get enough information to prove to her that the Bible was full of lies. However, as he read, something beautiful happened! The powerful two-edged sword of the Word cut at his heart. He was convicted of his sins and surrendered his life to Christ.

We drove about four hours from Baghdad to Erbil and checked into our hotel after going through very tight security screening. Only a few hours before this, Islamic radicals had bombed a nearby building, killing over twenty people. The hotel electricity was unreliable. The water flow was a trickle. The elevator was older than the nearby hills and made banging, clanging sounds that made everyone feel it would collapse at any moment. There were holes in the walls in the bedrooms; no housekeeping was available for the three days we were there.

About one hundred eighty pastors and other church leaders gathered for the training. Representing about eighty percent of the evangelical leadership in the nation, they gathered from cities from Mosul in the north to Basra in the south. One pastor, who stated that he leads one of only three evangelical churches in Basra (a city of two and a half million), drove almost six hundred miles to be with us, delayed by dozens of military checkpoints.

"I would have *walked* six hundred miles if necessary," he added. "I'm starving for biblical leadership training. We urgently need leaders to plant churches in our nation."

John, Randy, Phil, and I taught numerous lessons, but the leaders continued begging for more. Even as we tried leaving for the airport for our departure flight, they surrounded us, pleading for us to return and asking for Christian books in their language. None of us has ever taught a group more eager to learn.

When we arrived at the Erbil airport, monsoon-like rain was falling. The unpaved landing strip was rapidly becoming a quagmire. We were soon informed that our inbound flight could not land and was returning to Baghdad. We were offered two options. Both involved renting a couple of vehicles in Mosul (a very dangerous city located about an hour away). There was no assurance that vehicles would be available, and there was no way of knowing if local drivers were trustworthy. Another option was to drive seventeen hours through the desert to Amman, Jordan. The other was to drive five hours to Baghdad on "the most dangerous highway in the world," according to our Erbil friends. We chose the latter option.

Rany, our Egyptian colleague, was able to reach Air Serv in Amman by satellite phone and convince them to send a plane to Baghdad the following day to fly us to Jordan. Rany was able to locate two vehicles in Mosul, about an hour's drive from Erbil. Late in the afternoon we began our trek to Baghdad, arriving safely before midnight. Our route to Baghdad took us through Tikrit and only a few miles from the pit where Saddam was captured. The military checkpoints, staffed by U. S. Marines, were frequent. At one checkpoint we met a Marine from Atlanta, and Phil Orazi gave him a stack of Chick-fil-A gift coupons. I'm sure he received enough coupons to eat Chick-fil-A sandwiches free for the remainder of his life! This rugged-looking warrior grinned from ear to ear as he expressed his thanks to Phil.

As we drove into the outskirts of Baghdad, our Iraqi driver told Rany that a terrible bombing had occurred on our route earlier in the evening. Rany interpreted the message for us and explained that radicals had killed about two hundred Iraqis as they waited to enroll in the Iraqi military with intentions to cooperate with the American and British forces. A few minutes later, we saw the scene of the terrible tragedy that was caused earlier in the evening by terrorists detonating a car bomb. As promised, Air Serv took us the next day to Amman, where we had the joy of conducting a leadership conference for pastors and church leaders from Jordan, Syria, and Lebanon.

In Iraq the faces of persecuted Christians were etched permanently on my heart. I knew my life and ministry would never be the same!

Upon visiting Iran, I was deeply stirred by the testimonies of the house church leaders. The stories of how they came to Christ through dreams and visions, as well as through satellite television, will never be forgotten. We heard numerous reports that more Iranians had come to faith in Christ in the past fifteen years than in the previous *fifteen hundred* years. They expressed deep gratitude for the leadership training we have helped to provide.

The Lord has wonderfully blessed our first conferences in Cyprus and North Africa. We have served leaders from approximately fifteen nations with Islamic governments hostile to the gospel. These leaders are already training hundreds of other leaders back in their homelands. Many of these leaders serve in the most dark, dangerous, and difficult of places. What a joy to invest in their lives and ministries!

I must mention the special privilege God gave to Winnie and me to visit the Underground University, a partnership project in Seoul, South Korea. Men and women who have fled from North Korea because of the brutality of the regime or because of starvation, sometimes for both reasons, are studying EQUIP leadership lessons with a desire to return to the North to share the transforming message of Jesus Christ. Their testimonies live in our hearts and daily challenge us to give our best to serve persecuted Christians around the world.

Many of these North Koreans have shared stories of how they escaped the brutal dictatorship in their homeland. One lady told of her husband's imprisonment because he had made a negative comment about the North Korean ruler, and he had died in prison from starvation. She did her best to feed her family, but soon they were eating only tiny seeds like those that birds eat. They sometimes had only a few seeds for a full day— there was no other food. Her son became blind due to malnutrition and also because some of the seeds were poisonous. In desperation she helped her two daughters escape into China, where sadly, they became prostitutes in order to get money for food. Later she tried twice unsuccessfully to escape, once nearly drowning in a river and once caught by Chinese border guards and sent back to North Korea. When she made it to China on the third try, she was given shelter and food by Chinese house church believers who told her about Christ and helped her find her daughters and rescue them. They traveled through China and Burma, where they were imprisoned two years before being sent to Seoul. Today she is a vibrant, passionate Christian who is very grateful for Bible-based leadership training that has deepened her faith and given her a vision to evangelize in North Korea.

Our visit to Cambodia reminded us of how exceedingly evil dictatorial leaders are. We wept as we visited torture chambers and the killing fields where so many suffered because of the brutality of Pol Pot and his thugs. One of the young men whose head was bashed against a tree and then thrown with hundreds of dead bodies into a mass grave was able to escape during the night hours. Though badly wounded, he was able to walk under the cover of night until he escaped from Cambodia. We met him at his church, where he is now helping raise up a new generation of leaders for Cambodia. The Pol Pot regime had intentional slaughtered everyone they believed to be educated. They considered anyone who could read and write as enemies of the nation.

I traveled into Vietnam with a missionary who was a former American fighter pilot who had flown many bombing missions against the Vietcong. Now a devout follower of Christ, my missionary friend shared the love of Jesus in the nation where he had once dropped bombs. It was beautiful to watch him hugging the fifty or so pastors in the EQUIP leadership conference and lifting them one by one to the Lord in prayer.

A precious lady known for her prayer ministry also attended the training. We wept as she shared how soldiers from North Vietnam came to her home and killed her husband and sons with gunshots to the head. Their crime was simply having befriended American soldiers who were stationed in her village. She had extended forgiveness to those who took the lives of her loved ones. Her joy in Christ was amazing to behold!

Winnie and I are grateful to John and Larry Maxwell and the EQUIP board for the privilege of serving leaders around the globe. Wherever we have traveled, our lives have been impacted by the commitment and courage of men and women who are willing to give their lives for the sake of Jesus, their Redeemer and Lord.

We have also been wonderfully enriched by friendship with the generous men and women who currently serve on the EQUIP board of directors, as well as those who have previously served: Steve Miller, Collin Sewell, Chris Hodges, Kevin Myers, Ed Bastian, Tom Arington, Matt Eddy, Steve Robinson, Tom Mullins, Jim Blanchard, John Williams, Gerald Brooks, Chris Stephens, Dennis Rouse, Sarah Grace Wall, Larry Maxwell,

Ray Moats, Dave Anderson, Don Wilson, Chuck Harrison, Tami Heim, Sam Chand, Gil Scott, and others. They have set a superbly high standard of leadership and stewardship faithfulness and excellence. The faithful generosity of these individuals and their spouses has been a major reason for the sustained impact of EQUIP worldwide. I've had the joy of serving with three EQUIP presidents: Ron McManus, John Hull, and Tom Mullins, and many other very dedicated, talented colleagues.

We can never express how blessed we have been to build friendships in over a hundred nations. From successful business leaders in major cities to the poorest of the poor in remote villages around the world, it has been our joy to establish friendships that have challenged us to a closer walk with Christ and moved our hearts to greater generosity in serving others. Each one of the thousands of friends has a special story of how he or she came to faith in Christ and of His unfailing grace. Some of them are in our inner circle of closet friends.

Fung Ming Lim and his wife, Eileen, in Malaysia are in this group. After they experienced the impact of leadership training in their lives, they committed to use their time and resources to train and equip other leaders in Asia. In city after city in Malaysia and in other nations of the region, they have traveled at their own expense to pour biblical leadership training into the lives of hundreds of Christian men and women eager to make a maximum impact for Christ. Their son Jonathan named his oldest son in my honor. I pray daily that Douglas Lim will grow up to be a difference-maker for the glory of the Lord.

We look forward to the future of EQUIP. I pray daily for continued health and strength to serve the Lord Jesus and EQUIP with excellence and increased effectiveness. I'm blessed to serve with Rob McCleland, Mark Cole, and Tom Mullins. Karen Hartman, my executive assistant, is a very devout woman of faith and a special gift from the Lord. She shares my passion to serve our donors with excellence. I will always be grateful for the helpfulness of Linda Eggers and Linda Kirk. Both are devoted servants of Christ.

Even as Winnie and I pray for good health, we ask God for wisdom in how to balance our time commitments. In addition to training Christian leaders, we are passionate about our commitment to lovingly invest meaningful time in our children and grandchildren. We are blessed to have Angie and Shelby living nearby. We can see them almost daily, but we also have Jason in Indiana and Eric with his beautiful Stacy and their three precious little boys in Florida. Jackson is our oldest grandson, and his brothers are twins. We are determined to "be there" for Shelby, Jackson, Preston, and Landon as they grow up.

All three of our children enjoy participating in and watching sports. While we are quite divided in our college football and basketball allegiance, we have always agreed on the Dodgers and the Cowboys. All of us enjoy NASCAR, and Eric and Jason love golf. Shelby pulls for Peyton Manning wherever he is playing.

Election to the inaugural class of the EQUIP Leadership Hall of Fame was a high honor. The respect of my children, friends, and coworkers is a special treasure and genuinely appreciated. Hugs and kisses from our grandkids are even better. But when our earthly pilgrimage ends, Winnie and I desire to one day receive the highest honor of all—a hug from our heavenly Father as He whispers, "Well done, good and faithful servants." We are determined with God's help to finish well.

The Great Commission mandate burns brightly in our hearts. The following words from an anonymous source stand as a reminder of the urgency of the hour: "Our God of grace often gives us a second chance, but there is no second chance to harvest a ripe crop." As Jesus said, "Look on the fields; for they are white already to harvest" (John 4:35).

4

Global Ambassador for Christ 2015–2020

One of the highlights of 2015 was an exciting leadership conference and celebration held on the island of Fiji in the South Pacific in June. Winnie and I were abundantly blessed to be there. During this conference I was privileged to join John Maxwell, Dave Anderson, and others in teaching Million Leaders Mandate curriculum to key leaders from the island of Kiribati. As a result of the faithfulness and generosity of our prayer and financial partners, EQUIP had introduced biblical leadership training to every independent nation on earth—all one hundred ninety-six of them! From India in 1997 to Kiribati in 2015, millions of Christian leaders were trained.

It was an unexpected moment during this event when John asked my executive assistant, Karen Hartman, and me to join him on the platform. He very graciously presented us special gifts recognizing the many years we had served the constituents of EQUIP. I will always be deeply grateful to Karen for the wonderful support she has provided to me. Her prayers, her Christlike life, and her professional expertise have added immensely to the impact of EQUIP around the world.

In May 2016 the EQUIP team hosted the Associate Trainer Summit in Atlanta. Hundreds of men and women who had served as international volunteer trainers were honored for their faithful service worldwide. They had traveled countless miles and invested millions of dollars to add value to Christian leaders in one hundred ninety-six nations. Each associate trainer was presented a beautiful plaque expressing appreciation for his or her global impact. I was totally surprised when John handed the first award to me and explained that I had taught in more nations than any other trainer. As I expressed thanks for the plaque, I sincerely acknowledged all the trainers with special mention of George Clinton, Steve Miller, Sam Hoyt, and others who had served in many nations.

Early in 2017 the Salt & Light Conference was held in Duluth, Georgia (a few miles northeast of Atlanta). At this time John Maxwell cast vision for the Salt & Light Global Evangelism Initiative. This project will use roundtables (small groups) and leadership + evangelism curriculum to add value, build relationships, and share Christ around the world. Just as with the Million Leaders Mandate, volunteer associate trainers are playing a vital role around the world training roundtable hosts/leaders. John and the EQUIP team are expecting at least one million people to be reached for Christ by 2022 through roundtables—and one million reached each year thereafter!

One of the special moments in 2017 was the opportunity to deliver the commencement address at Ohio Christian University. As you will recall, I served as the president of this Christian institution for nine years (1980–1989) when it was known as Circleville Bible College. Renamed Ohio Christian University in 2007, the university experienced exponential growth under the superb leadership of Mark Smith. I will always admire his bold, visionary, innovative leadership.

Back on campus for graduation on April 29, 2017, I spoke on the subject "Running the Christian Race." My three key points were (1) begin with purpose, (2) run with patience, and (3) finish with passion.

After finishing my message to the graduates, I was in for quite a surprise! Dr. Smith awarded to me an honorary degree, doctor of divinity. I think I was the most shocked person alive that day. What a joy to be honored with a degree from the school I had served years before!

One of the heartbreaking moments in 2017 was the passing of Stan Toler. His widow, Linda, who is my niece, asked me to be one of the speakers at his Celebration of Life service at Bethany (Oklahoma) First Church of the Nazarene, where a huge crowd gathered December 8 to honor the life and ministry of Stan. Following is an excerpt from my remarks delivered that day:

> *Forty-seven years ago (1970) at the Taylor County Camp Meeting in central Georgia on a hot July day, my wife and I were the missionary speak-*

ers. There was a quartet singing in the service—a group of young preacher boys from Circleville Bible College (now Ohio Christian University). One of the lads was very small in size with a gracious smile and a perfect haircut. When the offering was received, he pledged to give $5.00 per month to our support in spite of the fact that he was paying his own way through college and struggling to survive financially. His name was Stan Toler. There is no amount of money that equals the value of his investments in my life, family, and ministry since that day.

Stan was always focused on others, never himself. He never sought recognition or praise. He tossed ego and logos aside because he never desired to have control or to receive credit. Servanthood and personal integrity—yes, Christlikeness—marked his life. Stan was always young at heart and small in size, but he was a giant of the Christian faith who impacted countless thousands for Christ around the world.

In 2017 I met with John Maxwell to discuss my transition from full-time to part-time with EQUIP in order for me to have more time for Winnie, our children, and our grandchildren. I highly recommended that my longtime friend R. D. Saunders be invited to serve as the chief development officer at EQUIP, a role I had filled since the birth of EQUIP in 1996.

I first met R. D. at Stoutsville Camp Meeting in Ohio in the early 1980s prior to his enrollment at Circleville Bible College. Our lives have been closely connected ever since. R. D. is doing an exceptionally good job as director of advancement at EQUIP.

I now continue one-fourth time with EQUIP—primarily in an advisory or consultative role to our leadership team. In December 2019 I celebrated my seventy-eighth birthday and marked twenty-three years of service with EQUIP.

I am also serving as a consultant with World Gospel Mission, where Dan Schafer is the president. I've had the joy of investing in Dan and working closely with him in Great Commission ministry for many years.

My dear friend, neighbor, and former colleague at EQUIP Michel Khalil launched a new nonprofit organization in 2017 for the specific purpose of providing leadership, discipleship, and evangelism training for key Christian leaders in the nations of the Middle East, North Africa, and the Gulf countries. Michel, who was born in Egypt, has lived in the Atlanta area since 1996, when he came to the city to do street evangelism during the Olympics. His wife, Roula, born in Lebanon, and their two daughters have become some of our dearest friends.

Michel is uniquely qualified to lead a ministry to the Middle East, North Africa, and the Gulf countries. In his early adult years back in Egypt he obediently responded to God's calling upon his life to missionary service. His beloved uncle was killed while witnessing to Muslims, and Michel harbored deep bitterness in his heart toward those who took the life of his loved one, but the grace of God enabled him to forgive even those who had caused him terrible pain. His God-given mission was to share Christ with those enslaved in the grip of Islam. His missionary work took him to Sudan, where he saw God changing many lives. Like many other missionaries there, he was arrested and deported. Once back in Egypt, he was placed under house arrest, which continued until he was able to migrate to America. After a brief stay in New York City, he relocated to Atlanta in 1996 just in time to be involved in street evangelism during the Summer Olympic Games.

Not long after the Olympics concluded, he began serving with Haggai Institute, an international ministry that conducts leadership training events overseas. It was during one of these conferences that he met Roula, a beautiful Christian young woman from Lebanon. Subsequently they were married and Roula joined Michel in the Atlanta area.

Michel's primary responsible with Haggai Institute was to host and coordinate training in the Arabic-speaking nations of the Middle East and Gulf countries. After fifteen years in this role, he felt God leading him to resign and "wait upon the Lord" for his next assignment. In 2012 I had the special joy of meeting Michel. Shortly thereafter, he became a member of the EQUIP team with major responsibilities in the office of international operations. He arranged conferences in the greater Middle East region and eventually coordinated EQUIP's Million Leaders Mandate in one hundred ninety-six nations.

When Michel left EQUIP in 2017, he asked me to serve as the board chairman of his new nonprofit organization, Step Forward Global Ministries. When accepting this role, I never dreamed that in 2018 alone I would be making eight trips to the Middle East, North Africa, and western Europe to invest in hundreds of Arabic-speaking leaders who are serving on the frontlines in dark, difficult, and dangerous places. The ministry continues growing in scope and impact, and I am grateful that God continues providing health and strength for me to serve alongside Michel and other volunteer teachers, including my longtime friends Pastor Steve Schellin and Dan Schafer. As a result of the Arab Spring and the current refugee crisis, there has been an opportunity for unprecedented spiritual harvest in this region. Thousands of Muslims are coming to Christ. The ministry of Step Forward could not be more strategic and timely.

The testimonies we hear stir our souls. The cost to follow Jesus is very difficult in nations where Islam is dominant. Suffering as a result of the brutality of Islam is widespread in the Middle East and North Africa. One young woman told of the beatings by her dad and brother when she gave her life to Jesus. They even kept her chained to a post in their house, releasing her only to use the toilet. She escaped one evening when freed to use the bathroom. Underground Christians found her almost dead in an alley. Today she is faithfully leading hundreds of Islamic young adults, including many university students, to a saving relationship with Christ.

Another pastor from an Islamic nation of North Africa told us how he and five men in his underground church were arrested and placed in one very small cell (about three feet by three feet). The cell was so small that the men were unable to even bend down to pick up the stale bread thrown on the floor daily by the guards. They were relieved to be outside their tiny cell occasionally, even if to be beaten.

Because of the Christlike spirit these prisoners maintained, the guards began asking how they could be so positive while in such terrible conditions. Upon hearing about Jesus, one of the guards gave his life to Him and secretly released them from the prison. The guard also escaped and became active in their church.

I recall a conversation with a pastor in one of the nations of the Arabian Gulf. He led to Christ a man from an almost one-hundred-percent Islamic nation where access is strictly controlled. After the new believer was given a Bible, he returned to his apartment and read the entire New Testament overnight. At 8:00 the next morning he returned to the pastor's door rejoicing in his newfound salvation and stated that he had to return to his homeland to tell his family about Jesus. The pastor cautioned him about the grave danger of trying to cross the border with a Bible in his possession.

He replied, "I must take the Book to my loved ones. They must know that Jesus loves them."

Six years later the man reappeared at his pastor's door rejoicing and praising Jesus, explaining that he had indeed re-

turned to his home country, where he was arrested and imprisoned for one year. After his release from prison, his passport
was taken for five years. As soon as he received a new passport,
he traveled immediately to the neighboring nation to let his
pastor know that he was living victoriously in Jesus in spite of
imprisonment, torture, and loss of his business.

I will never forget talking with a gentleman from Mau-
ritania who was participating in one of our conferences. He
had spent many years in slavery in his country, where about
twenty percent of the people live as slaves. He explained that
a missionary visited the area where he lived and talked with
the slaves and the slave owners about Jesus. (The missionary
was a church planter who has faithfully attended our leadership conferences.) Both he (the slave) and the master (the slave
owner) gave their hearts to Christ, and immediately the master
decided to grant emancipation to his slave.

You can imagine the slave's joy as he experienced freedom
twice the same day—freedom from his earthly master and freedom from the bondage of sin! The former slave and his former
master began to doing ministry together. The former master
even gave the former slave the room in which the master's own
son had once lived. "You are no longer a slave," he said. "Instead, you are my brother in Christ and also my adopted son."

The two have shared Jesus and His love with thousands
of masters and slaves. Many slaves in their region have experienced the same double types of deliverance.

A senior pastor, an associate pastor, and several lay people of
a church in Beirut, Lebanon, participated in leadership train-

ing in the Middle East. The senior pastor commented, "When I first attended the leadership training conference and made a commitment to train leaders in my congregation of eighty members (about two hundred attendees), little did I know that transformation would take place in my church, that God was preparing us for a great harvest of souls as refugees began flooding into our city from Iraq and Syria and that hundreds would be reached for Christ. Little did I know that in two years our church would grow from two hundred people to eleven hundred families."

It has been my joy to preach numerous times in this church. You can imagine my joy when informed that I would have the opportunity to share the gospel message with several hundred Iraqi and Syrian refugees, all Muslims, during two services on a Monday evening. The response to the salvation message was beautiful as scores came forward to invite Christ into their hearts. We prayed, we wept, and we enjoyed Christian fellowship with new Christ-followers. Many shared testimonies of the transforming power of the gospel when they believed.

I love teaching in the conferences arranged by Michel Khalil in a variety of locations in the greater Middle East region of the world. Each conference brings together key leaders from several nations of the Middle East and/or North Africa. What a special joy to invest in the lives of the dedicated men and women who serve on frontlines of Christian ministry in areas where they daily face the harshness and brutality of Islam!

It has also been a special privilege to preach the gospel in this region. I am so blessed to have Michel serve as my interpreter when I preach. He shares my passion for communicating the good news effectively under the anointing of the Holy Spirit.

International audiences love stories, I have learned, including Bible stories. God has graciously used the story of the feeding of the five thousand to communicate how He works mightily through the obedience of even a lad who gave his best to Jesus. The "4-H Club" (Helpless, Healer, Helpers, and Hinderers) in Mark 2 has challenged many to get involved in bringing people to Jesus. The story of Abraham and Isaac, "Is Your Isaac on the Altar?" has called many to a full surrender to the lordship of Christ.

In January 2019 I joined Michel and others in a historic meeting in Cairo with the head of the Coptic Orthodox Church. This two-thousand-year-old denomination has about twenty-two million members worldwide (eighteen million in Egypt), but only about three million are faithful. The top officials reported that the leadership training we have provided has ignited a spiritual renewal movement in the denomination with a special focus on evangelism and discipleship. Step Forward has been given an invitation to train as many church leaders as we possibly can. In the spring of 2019 Michel and I ministered in Morocco, nation number 128, where I have had the joy of representing our Lord.

When Winnie and I moved back to our home state of Georgia in 1997, we greatly missed our children, who remained in Indiana. In 2001 our daughter, Angie; her husband; and one-year-old Shelby, our only granddaughter, moved near us in the Atlanta area. Angie is now the principal of a large public elementary school in our county. Beautiful Shelby is now enrolled at the University of North Georgia.

Meanwhile, our son Eric moved to Orlando to pursue his career in emergency medicine. He married a sweet, beautiful Floridian, Stacy, and they have three handsome sons: Jackson, Landon, and Preston. Winnie and I love visiting them in Florida every couple of months.

Jason continues living in Marion, Indiana. After several years teaching elementary school, he is now pursuing his dream to work in the food service industry. He is managing a restaurant—and loves it.

I know that none of us selected our parents or where we were born. As Winnie and I have traveled the world and witnessed firsthand the suffering and sadness in so many nations and in countless families, we repeatedly thank God for our upbringing by Christian parents who loved us unconditionally and faithfully endeavored to teach us traditional biblical values. Also, we are grateful for brothers and sisters who loved us and shared our dreams to always live Christ-centered lives.

Over the years I have had the joy of conducting countless weddings for our nephews and nieces as well as other relatives and friends. On the other hand, I never anticipated that over the past couple decades I would say good-bye to my wonderful sisters—Johnnie, Mary Kathryn, and Marguerite—and my only brother, James M. (Buddy) Carter. I spoke at the funeral of each of them, as well as the funerals of several nephews and other relatives.

Winnie was one of ten siblings: five boys and five girls. Eight of them are now deceased. I spoke at the funerals of most of them as well. Winnie's sister Willie is her only remaining sibling. Because of declining health, Willie has recently moved to South Carolina to live with her son, Steve, and his wife, Janet. When Winnie and I recently drove into Alma, our hometown, we suddenly realized that for the first time in our lives we had no brothers or sisters living there. Of course, we were comforted by the assurance that our parents and our brothers and sisters are now living in the heavenly city.

I am forever grateful for my godly wife, her unconditional love and powerful ministry of prayer, hundreds of generous friends, and Jesus, my Savior, Sanctifier, and coming King! Even though Winnie has struggled with high blood pressure in recent years, she has been able to travel overseas often with me. Every journey is more meaningful and fulfilling when she is by my side; but on those occasions when it is necessary for her to remain at home, what a blessed joy to know that she is faithfully interceding for me in prayer! She seems to have a special hotline to the Lord.

One of the highlights of the summer of 2019 was attending the annual indoor camp meeting of the West Central District of the Churches of Christ in Christian Union. A special invitation to this gathering was extended to Winnie and me because the 1983 "Maranatha" singing group would be doing a reunion concert on Sunday evening during the encampment. More than thirty-five years had passed since these talented young men and women had traveled together during their years at Circleville Bible College (now Ohio Christian University). Winnie and I were so excited to be there to hear them sing some of our favorite gospel songs. We were not disappointed! As was always the case, the Holy Spirit powerfully anointed the music ministry of Shelli Brown Saunders, Susan Long Jones, Denise Knisley, and Bruce Morrison. They invited Shelli's husband, R. D., to join them on a couple of songs. Winnie and I enjoyed every moment of the concert. Precious memories flooded our hearts and tears of joy flowed down our faces!

Following the concert, the camp meeting service began under the direction of District Superintendent Joe Duvall. Neither Winnie nor I had any idea that she and I, along with our very dear friends David and Sally Case, would be given special recognition during the service. We were shocked when Rev. Duvall called us to the platform and began reading very gracious words of introduction for the four of us. Pastor Steve McGuire offered words of tribute to Dr. and Mrs. Case and presented a beautiful plaque to them. My longtime friend and colleague at EQUIP Leadership, R. D. Saunders, "outdid himself" with a beautiful tribute to Winnie and me before he handed us the very nice plaque from the West Central District, which contained the following words:

In honor of your godly example, your faithful investment in God's people, your commitment to biblical truth and teaching of sound doctrine, your wise and endearing counsel, patience, and compassion, your leadership and fortitude, but most importantly, your love and friendship, please accept our deepest gratitude and most sincere expression of thanks.

In each key leadership role God handed to me through the years, I always endeavored to do my very best to invest effectively in others and to create a culture that inspired personal growth for everyone and motivated the team to stay focused on a clear and compelling vision. During our years at Southwest Indian School, God enabled us to construct numerous urgently needed buildings. My priorities at Circleville Bible College were to increase salaries for faculty and staff and to grow the endowed scholarship funds. It was a big victory for students who resided in Ohio when the state legislature approved our participation in the state's Basic Educational Opportunity Grant program.

I thank God for every opportunity to serve the missionaries of World Gospel Mission, from 1989 through 1996. It was a special joy to lead the establishment of the Office of Advancement and to design and implement the Support Development Institute, special training to help missionaries build their personal support teams.

The upgrade and modernization of facilities, including installation of air conditioning in the M. J. Wood Memorial Tabernacle, was one of my special dreams for Taylor County Camp Meeting. I thank God for the generosity of His faithful people who made this dream—and so much more—become a reality. To Him I give praise always! In an era when many camp meetings have struggled to survive and some have closed, God has kept Taylor County strong.

Perhaps the most challenging and rewarding of all was the privilege of serving as the first employee of EQUIP Leadership, founded in 1996 by John Maxwell. My one-man development department was overwhelmed with one huge question: "Where do I begin?" As a new organization, we had no impact stories to tell. I began sharing the vision of John and Larry Maxwell to see effective leaders fulfilling the Great Commission in every nation, traveling far and wide communicating our mission to train and equip Christian leaders to reach the nations for Christ. Although we had no success stories to share when we began, a God-given vision burned within. John Maxwell and I invited others to join us on this amazing journey to develop godly servant-leaders around the world. The response was overwhelmingly positive. We certainly did not know in those days that by 2015 EQUIP would have impacted the lives of Christian leaders in every nation on our planet!

I recall those early days of traveling overseas with John with a camera for still photos as well as a huge video camera draped around my neck. I kept a pad in my pocket on which I wrote the story of each person I met who was hungry for leadership training. I had a briefcase full of battery packs and camera cords. Strategy meetings, training sessions, and relationship-building filled the day from early morning to late night. There was little time for rest. Our vision gave passion, and the passion produced energy to keep going.

I had the joy of traveling with John to many nations. A trip with him often included audiences with high-level leaders in church, business, and government—even presidents, prime ministers, and members of parliaments. On the other hand, there were frequent visits with the poorest of the poor, the unloved, and the marginalized. I will never forget walking with pastors who were investing their lives reaching out to the outcasts struggling to survive in the slums of many major international cities. I thank God for His servants who are serving those who live in the "garbage dumps" on the outskirts of these huge urban areas.

I think often of the pastor in the slums of an African city with an entire congregation of women who were dying with AIDS because of unfaithful husbands. After I preached in the little building constructed with a few pieces of rusty tin with a dirt floor and no roof, several ladies asked me to offer special prayer for them. With huge smiles and expressions of joy and gratitude, they told me of their love for the Lord and gratitude for their salvation. On the other hand, they wept with broken hearts as they asked for prayer for their children. Some of the children suffered with AIDS while others were deathly sick from dysentery cause by the lack of clean water. The pastor said he conducted funerals for infants and children every week.

It was always the mission of EQUIP to invest in God's servants on the frontlines of Christian ministry around the world, whether in major cities or in tiny villages in remote regions of the neediest nations on our planet. I will forever be grateful to John Maxwell for the invitation to take this journey with him. I deeply appreciate the EQUIP presidents—Ron McManus, John Hull, Tom Mullins, and Terence Chatmon—with whom I have served. I am praying daily for Founder and Board Chairman John Maxwell, CEO Mark Cole, Executive Director George Hoskins, and Director of Development R. D. Saunders as they continue leading EQUIP in mobilizing Christian leaders to reach the nations for Christ. I am confident that in the years immediately ahead, EQUIP will help unleash a worldwide movement reaching millions for Christ.

The rapid growth of Step Forward is amazing. It has been an overwhelming blessing to volunteer my time to help my friend Michel Khalil with the launch and expansion of this ministry that is focused on serving persecuted Christians in the Middle East and North Africa.

My report on one of the conferences in North Africa follows:

I'm writing this report on Tuesday, September 17, 2019, as I'm flying home from North Africa via Paris to Atlanta. It was indeed a blessed privilege to again invest in church leaders from several nations of North Africa. The conference was beautifully organized and directed by Michel Khalil, the president of Step Forward. I taught alongside Rev. Bruce Morrison, Dr. Sam Hoyt, and Dr. Dan Schafer. Each of us sensed a beautiful spirit of oneness and divine anointing as we taught biblical truth. Each session was focused on a key component of discipleship. The Holy Spirit graciously ministered to all our hearts in every session over three days of training. It was an added joy to have Elaine Hoyt and Pam Schafer with us as our special prayer warriors.

About noontime on the first day of the conference we learned that eleven police officers had arrived at our hotel to "investigate" us. We were later told that when the police commissioner sends that number of officers, they fully intend to make arrests. The officers confronted our local travel agent (a Muslim) about the teachers, attendees, and content of our training. Someone had told them we were teaching a false religion.

With utmost integrity he explained that we were in full compliance with the laws of the nation. He explained that we were not evangelizing on the street corners (forbidden by law) but meeting with other believers to teach Christian principles (permitted under the new constitution).

He defended our integrity and the truth of our teachings.

We were praying. Many others in America and in the Middle East region were doing the same. God heard and answered! The Lord God "turned their hearts." Before the encounter ended, the top officer gave assurance that several officers would be nearby to protect us from anyone who tried to hinder or interrupt the training.

That evening Michel received a warning of threats against him. The matter was quickly resolved the next day. The conference proceeded without further incidents.

The Holy Spirit was clearly evident in every session. The prayer times and praise and worship times were wonderful as God ministered so powerfully and faithfully to every attendee. We wrapped up the last day with forty minutes of prayer. Revival fires burned in our hearts. Glorious moments! All of us (teachers and students, over forty of us) were praying and seeking a fresh outpouring of His Spirit. God came! It was beautiful.

The efforts of the enemy to stop the conference failed. To God be praise now and forever. This may have been our best discipleship conference ever!

All attendees were converts from Islam. Many were quite new believers, but they had already been tested in the fires of persecution. Many had experienced beatings by other members of their families and been tossed out of their homes because of their decision to follow Christ. Some had been imprisoned while others were refused employment simply because they dared to tell others about Jesus. All of them are passionate and effective soul-winners. All were hungry to study the Word of God, to grow spiritually, and to learn how to effectively disciple those they are leading to Jesus in the dark, difficult, and dangerous places where they live, serve, and courageously share their faith every day.

Dr. Khalil, who directed the conference, and we who had the joy of teaching received lots of hugs and saw many tears of gratitude. I wish you—you who have prayed and given—could have heard the comments. One young pastor exclaimed, "This is exactly what I needed!" He explained that he had learned so very much and that his heart had experienced revival. He commented that he would never be the same, that he is refreshed, renewed, and refueled. He added, "Please come back soon to pour into our hearts and minds." He asked us to pray for him and the other church leaders. I never heard him ask for prayer for safety, but he pleaded with us to ask God to give them boldness to continue speaking the name of Jesus whatever the cost. This is the urgent request from all of them.

The following testimony was shared with me by one of the conference attendees. For security reasons I will omit his name and the country of North Africa in which he lives and serves.

He explained that his father was a very committed Muslim, as were most people in his area of his homeland. In fact, many extremists still live there. Most women wear coverings (burkas) for their faces.

His father's first wife died when his father was sixty. He re-married and then the man sharing this testimony was born. His older half-brothers hated him, and when he was a small lad his brothers threw him from the top of a tall tree trying to kill him. He survived, severely injured. When he was seventeen the older brothers convinced their dad to make him leave home. From early childhood his father had wanted nothing to do with him and refused to pay for him to attend even elementary school.

When he left home at seventeen, he immediate began drinking heavily and growing drug plants in the little shack where he lived. He began selling drugs and illegal guns. He became very wicked doing anything to make money.

At age twenty-five he was almost killed, so he thought he would go to the mosque seeking help. One afternoon, fully awake, he had a vision of a mosque with a black veil over the entrance. When anyone entered the mosque, the veil seemed to swallow him or her into a hole of darkness. He heard a voice he believed to be God saying that the mosque could never help him. Discouraged, he took the remains of his drug money and went to the casino and soon became a heavy gambler.

A few months later he began wondering about the voice he had heard speak so audibly to him about the mosque and wondered if God really existed. Walking one evening around 10:00 PM, he saw a man walking toward him. It was an uncle whom he had not seen in years. As they talked, he told his uncle about the voice. The uncle said that three months earlier he had met the true God at a small house church, handed him a small booklet, and urged him to read it.

Rather than going to the casino to gamble away the night as usual, he went home and began reading the little book—the gospel of Luke. When he came to the Lord's Prayer, he fell on his knees with his face to the floor and began praying over and over the prayer that Jesus taught His disciples. He finished reading Luke about 6:00 AM.

He then went to find his uncle. It was Friday, the day for church, and he begged his uncle to take him to church. The uncle was afraid, fearing he was only serving as a spy. After all, for eight years he had been a very wicked and dangerous man. However, he continued begging his uncle to take him to church, explaining that he had read Luke, prayed the Lord's Prayer, and genuinely wanted to meet the true God.

His uncle relented. At church the young man heard the people singing, praying, and calling God their Father, and he began weeping. They said God loved them. His own father had never loved him, never even let him eat in his presence, seldom ever spoken to him. The god of Islam had certainly never shown any love to him. But now he was hearing about a God who is a loving Father. He heard the voice again, and it said, "You can know the Father through His Son, Jesus." He went forward for prayer, invited Jesus into his life, and was transformed.

As he was approaching his little shack of a home after church, he saw a dove at his front door. He expected it to fly away as always when a human approached. But it didn't. He assumed it was injured and so he reached down to pick up the bird. As he lifted it, a powerful burning sensation coursed through both arms and to his heart. It was like a fire but was comforting. He felt his heart beginning to burn with the love of God the Father. He knelt, wept, and gave praise to His Heavenly Father.

After running to his father and mother's home, he expressed regret to them for his years of wickedness and asked forgiveness for the shame he had brought to his family, sharing that he had been totally changed by Jesus Christ. He begged his eighty-five-year-old father to meet Jesus.

His father responded, "I'll speak with you about Jesus if you are still a changed man two years from now."

The young man quit smoking, drinking, and gambling that day and destroyed the drug plants growing in his house. He never looked back to the old life. He was forever changed.

He became very active in the local house church, where the pastor noticed that he was very faithful to read and learn the Word of God. He noticed that he was growing spiritually very quickly. The pastor began taking him deeper in the Word and providing personal mentoring to him.

The young man began immediately sharing his testimony and winning souls. His pastor encouraged him to start a church in the larger house that had been purchased. One of the Muslim young women he invited to church soon gave her heart to Jesus. After she was baptized and well established in her new faith, they married.

This man is now thirty-nine, the couple has three children, and he has now been a Christian fourteen years, with ten years leading a church. His passion remains to win souls. In 2017 his father died at age 98. Not long before his death he gave his heart to Christ and died celebrating his victory in Jesus. His son wept as he shared about the day he led his father to a saving relationship with Christ.

The region where he lives is very dark, difficult, and dangerous. However, "Many are daily giving their hearts to Jesus," he explained with a big smile while weeping tears of joy.

He ended by emphasizing several times how much the Step Forward conference meant to him, explaining that he had learned a lot and that his heart had experienced revival and he would never be the same. "This was exactly what I needed!" he stressed, adding that he is refreshed, renewed, and refueled.

This excited, motivated believer asked that we pray for him and his associates as they share Jesus with the lost, that they would never cease to share the gospel, whatever the personal risk or cost.

I'm humbly grateful to God for the opportunities He gives my colleagues and me to invest in the lives and ministries of His faithful servants. Whether serving those who live and minister in dark and dangerous places overseas or investing in young leaders here at home, my heart is full of praise for the privilege.

From time to time I receive notes that remind me of the multiplied impact of investing in others. The wife of the pastor of a healthy, growing church in the Midwest sent me these words recently:

There are no words to thank you enough for all you have done for my husband. He grew up without a godly father, but then our faithful Heavenly Father placed you in his life. He is today a messenger of Jesus Christ because of you. You taught him, you loved him, and you mentored him. And you continue to do so!

A couple of days ago I received a card from a young associate pastor after I had spoken to his pastoral team in a staff retreat. He kindly wrote,

We just returned from our staff retreat, and I want you to know that our team has not stopped talking about the impact of your presentation. Many of our leaders have been in tears as they have reflected about renewed vision, revived faith, and refueled passion. Your encouragement was exactly what this weary team needed in this season of ministry.

You were so gracious to take time to drive so far to lift up our heads to see a greater vision. You so effectively reminded us that God has a unique way of replenishing our energy as we serve others for the kingdom. I watched you live out that truth as you stood in front of our team and poured out love upon us for two and a half hours. We are so very grateful and are praying for buckets of God's holy love to be poured out of you. We love you always.

Winnie and I are always aware of the hand of God upon our lives and deeply grateful for His favor. Likewise, we daily thank God for the wonderful friends who have faithfully supported and encouraged us with their love, prayers, and financial investments. Recently I came across a note I had written to some of our ministry partners in April 2019. Let me share here a portion of that letter:

> *During the more than fifty-five years that Winnie and I have been privileged to be involved in ministry, the Lord has opened to us amazing doors to serve the body of Christ worldwide. Only God could have used two kids—high school sweethearts from south Georgia—as His ambassadors to share the Good News around the world.*
>
> *While all praise goes to our wonderful Lord for His favor and blessings, we are genuinely grateful to you and others who have stood heart to heart with us on this journey of faith and obedience. Winnie and I are certain that your prayers and generosity have made—and continue to make—an eternal difference.*
>
> *We thank God for the key leaders who have influenced our lives and for the wonderful organizations that have provided us opportunities for global ministry. For example, through EQUIP I was blessed to serve the underground church in China for well over a decade. More recently God has used*

my friend, neighbor, and ministry partner Brother Michel Khalil to ignite in my heart a passion to serve the persecuted church in the Middle East and North Africa. As a result of the Arab Spring and the refugee crisis, the doors are currently open for unprecedented spiritual harvest in this dark, difficult, and dangerous region.

Winnie and I pray that God will give us many more years to serve Him together. On May 7 of the year this book is being published, 2020, we celebrated sixty years of marriage!

As I look back over the years of my life, I am so deeply grateful for the hand of the Lord upon me. I can't help but recall a couple of special moments when God used the words of others to remind me of the crucial importance of His guiding and empowering presence every moment.

During my childhood and adolescent years the local schools were still segregated; however, the workplace was largely integrated. In our community the workplace was primarily farms. I recall my first day picking cotton. I was in my early teens with no experience in the cotton field. A very gracious African American lady taught me how to pick cotton. I will never forget how she sang one gospel song after another as she gathered the cotton. She never once complained about the hard work or the extreme heat. At the end of the day the farmer weighed the cotton each of us had picked. I had picked about four hundred pounds—but she had picked *fifteen* hundred pounds, enough for a bale of cotton! In amazement that she had harvested so much cotton, I asked her, "How did you do that?"

Her reply inspires me yet today: "I didn't work alone. The hand of my Lord guided my hands and fingers. He's my helper."

Likewise, wherever I go and whatever I am called upon to do, I remember Brother Wood standing beside me with his arm around my shoulders as I endeavored to preach my first sermon back in 1959. Just as my pastor did, the Helper—the Holy Spirit—has throughout my life graciously and faithfully wrapped His arms about me and reminded me that I am not alone. I have prayerfully tried to make my ministry each day a *duet* with the Holy Spirit—never a solo.

When Piedmont Airlines Flight 486 was falling from the sky that spring day in 1988, I briefly wondered what would be said at my funeral. I quickly realized that earthly awards, trophies, and honors would mean nothing. I found myself praying, "Dear God, my utmost desire is that those who know me best can say honestly, 'In his life I saw Jesus.'" This remains the passionate prayer of my heart every day.

I often recall the words I muttered to myself decades ago when Pastor Wood stated that I would teach and preach in many nations around the world. In unbelief I whispered, "Not a chance." God surely had other plans. To Him I give thanks and praise forevermore!

5

Photo Gallery

Doug at about age 6

Doug's dad, Floyd M. Carter (April 17, 1894 – December 24, 1952)

Doug's mother, Mrs. Vera Douglas Carter (April 3, 1904 – May 30, 1984)

Doug (age 4) and sister Johnnie (age 1)

Wedding day, May 7, 1960, at Evangelistic Temple (now First Nazarene) in Alma, Georgia

(L to R) Adam, Linda, Seth, and Stan Toler. Linda is Doug's niece. Stan was one of Doug's spiritual heroes.

The Carter kids – (L to R) Angie, Eric, and Jason – October 2004

Just married. Douglas Marion and Winnie Orvin Carter cutting the wedding cake.

Doug played high school football in Alma, Georgia (1956–1959)

Beautiful Winnie Orvin played high school basketball 1956–1959. Her team won the Georgia State Championship in March 1959, and she captured Doug's heart the same year.

Winnie's parents, Alexis Ray and Ella Mae Orvin

(L to R) Doug, Jason, Winnie, Eric, and Angie (1990s in Gas City, Indiana)

Angela (Angie) Carter and Bart Gardner (students at Circleville Bible College)

(L to R) Angie, Doug, Winnie, Jason, and Eric (1980s in Circleville, Ohio)

Doug preached the funeral message for Native friend Erwin Patricio, in 2001

(L to R) Eric, Doug, Winnie, Jason, and Angie at Southwest Indian School (1978)

Doug was elected superintendent of Southwest Indian School in 1965.

Doug with Navajo student Roy Nells

Winnie with Native American student Benny Pintor

Doug became president of CBC/OCU in 1980.

Winnie and Doug

Doug and Winnie at Circleville Bible College (now Ohio Christian University). Doug was president 1980–1989.

(L to R) Rick and Sondra Atkinson with Winnie and Doug at installation of Doug as new member of city council in Gas City, Indiana

Jason Carter (age 1) is dedicated by Pastor Erwin Patricio at Southwest Indian School in 1979.

(L to R) Doug, Jason, Winnie, Eric, and Angie with Linda, Seth, and Stan Toler at Southwest Indian School (1978)

Doug and Winnie at EQUIP Leadership, Atlanta, Georgia, in 2001

Doug teaches in Lebanon with Michel Khalil.

Doug meets in Cairo, Egypt, with Pope of Coptic Orthodox Church.

Doug's book Big Picture People *is released in Arabic. Doug signs a copy for his Lebanese friend Sawsan Haddad.*

Doug's friend Michel Khalil interprets for him during one of their many trips together to the Arabic-speaking world.

Doug and Winnie's dear friend Mrs. Joseph Curley on the Navajo Reservation in Arizona

(L to R) AIM missionary pilot with Doug, Tom Hermiz, and Richard Adkins in Tanzania

Doug with a Maasai tribesman in Kenya

Doug visits with Ernie Steury, MD, at Tenwek Hospital in Kenya. Dr. Steury was a missionary doctor for many years with WGM.

Doug and Dr. O. D. Lovell, CBC professor, at the empty tomb near Jerusalem

Doug's friend Nathan Maher interprets for him in Egypt.

Doug with his siblings (L to R) Marguerite, Mary Kathryn, James M. "Buddy," Doug, and Johnnie

Doug's Siblings

(L to R) Doug, Buddy, Johnnie, Mary Kat, and Marguerite

John Maxwell welcomes Doug into the EQUIP Leadership Hall of Fame in 2012.

Elizabeth, a dear friend, with Winnie in China

Our wonderful friends Eileen and her husband, Lim Fung Ming, in Malaysia

Lim Fung Ming and Eileen's grandson Douglas Lim was named in Doug's honor.

Doug and Winnie in Bavaria (southern Germany) in 2010

Doug and Winnie with their beloved Navajo friends Charlotte and Dale Tsosie

Winnie's friend Elizabeth with Winnie in Shanghai, China

Winnie and Doug with their dear friend Louis Goh, who resides in Singapore

Doug's induction to EQUIP Leadership Hall of Fame: (L to R) Jason, granddaughter Shelby, Angie, Doug, Winnie, Eric, and Eric's wife, Stacy

Rev. M. J. Wood, founding pastor of the Evangelistic Temple in Alma, Georgia, and Doug's spiritual mentor

Quartet sings Southern gospel song at Taylor County Camp Meeting, Butler, Georgia. Doug was camp president for 25 years.

Winnie (center) with Dale and Charlotte Tsosie at a Southwest Indian School reunion

Winnie and Doug at an EQUIP event in Guatemala

Winnie keeping books at the Southwest Indian School in the 1960s

(L to R) Jason, Angie, Doug, Winnie, and Eric at Doug's induction ceremony for EQUIP Leadership Hall of Fame

Doug and a friend from a limited access nation

Doug teaches in Cyprus

(L to R) Sam and Elaine Hoyt, Pam and Dan Schafer, Bruce Morrison, and Doug in Tunisia

Doug and friends from a limited access nation

Doug teaching in Greece

John Maxwell honors Doug's longtime executive assistant, Karen Hartman, and Doug at an EQUIP training event in the Fiji Islands.

Doug and the EQUIP team celebrate reaching the goal of training leaders in all nations.

David Dean, Doug, and and a friend from a limited access nation

Doug's friend and longtime Indiana state representative Eric Turner, on behalf of Indiana Governor Mike Pence, presents the Sagamore of the Wabash award to Doug in January 2015

DOUGLAS M. CARTER

Doug Carter was EQUIP®'s first employee and currently serves as its Executive Director. He oversees day-to-day operations and represents the organization worldwide. Over the years, he has helped raise over $60 million for EQUIP®. He is an outstanding communicator who has ministered in more than 100 nations. John Maxwell calls Doug "Mr. EQUIP" because he so embodies the mission of the organization.

EQUIP Leadership Hall of Fame display in EQUIP offices in Duluth, Georgia

A plaque of appreciation

A plaque of appreciation

A plaque of appreciation

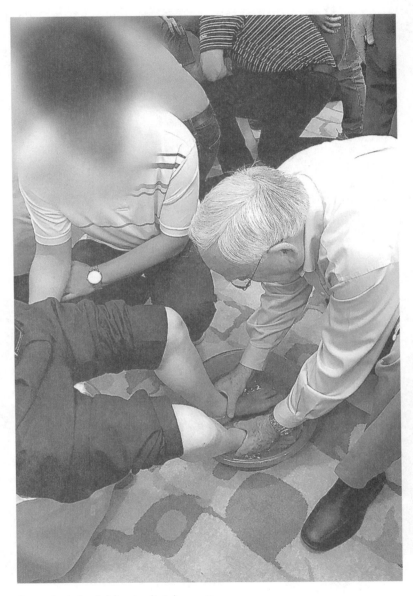

Doug washes the feet of a believer in a limited access nation.

Doug embraces a believer in a limited access nation.

Doug and coworker Michel Khalil on the Great Wall of China

Enjoying a fabulous meal in the home of Roula Khalil's parents, our dear and wonderful friends in Lebanon

Doug and Winnie with Roula's parents, Mr. and Mrs. Haddad

Michel and Doug teaching in the Middle East

Doug and Michel praying with refugees in Lebanon

Doug teaching in a Lebanese house church

Doug and Winn in Dubai, United Arab Emirates

Winnie and Doug with John and Margaret Maxwell at a Christmas gathering

Doug gives a Bible to a new believer in Paraguay.

Our beautiful Angie (R) with her beautiful Shelby, our only granddaughter

Doug prays at the Western Wall in Jerusalem

Shelby, our granddaughter, with her Big Papa Doug

R. D. Saunders and Doug are dearest friends and coworkers at EQUIP. When R. D. was a high school senior in Ohio, Doug recruited him to CBC.

Younger son, Jason, and Doug at Pebble Beach, California

Older son, Eric, is with his beautiful wife, Stacy, and their sons: (L to R) Landon, Jackson, and Preston. Landon and Preston are twins.

(L to R) Winnie, Landon, Doug, Preston, and Jackson. It is always a joy to be with our grandsons, who live in the Orlando area.

Willie Ree Altman, age 84, is Winnie's only living sibling of her five brothers and four sisters.

Our son Eric and his boys

Doug preaches the gospel in the Middle East.

Doug leading a service at the Taylor County Camp Meeting, Butler, Georgia. Doug surrendered his heart to Christ here in the summer of 1958.

Angie and Shelby in Germany in 2019

Doug delivers the graduation address at Ohio Christian University in 2017.

Doug and Winnie are all smiles as President Mark Smith and the trustees of Ohio Christian University give Doug an honorary Doctor of Divinity degree.

Doug visits Egypt with his friend Michel Khalil, the founder of Step Forward Global Ministries. Doug serves as chairman of the board of Step Forward.

Doug weeps as John Maxwell honors him for 23 years of service with EQUIP.

Doug and several friends pray with a refugee lady as she asks Christ to be her Savior.

Winnie and Doug, high school sweethearts, celebrated 60 years of marriage on May 7, 2020.

Doug's girls in Waco, Texas: (L to R) Angela, Shelby, and Winnie